SLOVAKIA

TRAVEL GUIDE
2024

Slovakia Unbound: Crafting Memories in the
Heart of Europe - Your 2024 Journey Begins

Philip Mablood

TABLE OF CONTENTS

Your Next Adventure Awaits

1. Introduction

Welcome to Slovakia:

Unraveling the Heart of Europe's Hidden Gem
A land of magic and exploration, Slovakia is waiting for you, tucked away in the center of Europe. You are about to set out on a voyage that is beyond time, weaving history, nature, and culture into an enthralling tapestry, as soon as you set foot on its rich soil. Greetings from Slovakia, a country rich in character, beauty, and resiliency, where each cobblestone street, mountain top, and filling meal narrates a tale.

A Symphony of Landscapes

Slovakia is a nation that skillfully combines many landscapes to create a symphony that will stay in your memory. With their peaks extending into the sky like sentinels defending the country, the High Tatras proudly stand as the jewel in the crown. This natural wonder is enhanced by deep forests, meandering rivers, and picture-perfect alpine lakes.

Step outside the mountains and you'll find yourself in the hiking and natural enthusiasts' paradise that is Slovak Paradise National Park. Poets and painters have been inspired by the lush valleys and attractive scenery that the

Danube River creates as it meanders throughout the nation for generations.

Whether you are drawn to the Slovak Karst's undulating hills or Pieniny National Park's serene beauty, each area begs you to explore, take in the clean air, and lose yourself in the unadulterated beauty that is Slovakia.

Whispers of History

Slovakia's past is enshrined in its picturesque towns, cobblestone squares, and medieval castles. The majestic silhouette of Bratislava Castle serves as a reminder of bygone eras as you stroll through the capital city's winding lanes. Explore the historic districts of Trnava and Košice, where the nation's rich legacy is reflected in the Gothic and Baroque buildings.

Tours to medieval castles will take you back in time to the era of knights and monarchs, letting you discover the remnants of the past within the stone walls. Slovakia sits at a crossroads of cultures due to its advantageous position, and its history demonstrates the tenacity of its people.

Cultural Revelry

Slovakia is a vibrant cultural tapestry full of customs and festivities, not just a blank canvas of breathtaking natural beauty. During festivals, the sounds of folk music fill the air, uniting communities in joyful harmony. Take part in the joy of traditional dances and savor the hand-crafted local cuisine that has been passed down through the years.

Slovakia's galleries and museums provide a more in-depth look into the country's creative spirit. Every institution tells a different part of the history of the country, whether it is through exhibits of ancient items or modern exhibitions. Take in the alluring fusion of the old and the new, where tradition and modernity coexist gracefully.

A Gastronomic Odyssey

Without sampling Slovakia's delectable cuisine, a trip there wouldn't be complete. Rich tastes and regional ingredients are celebrated in traditional Slovak cooking. Enjoy the national cuisine, bryndzové halušky, or the delicate layers of a traditional pastry, trdelník, while strolling through quaint marketplaces.

The vineyard-covered landscapes, where the rich history of winemaking is revealed with every drink, will provide joy to wine connoisseurs. Slovakia's wine areas, like the Small Carpathians and Tokaj, invite you to experience the distinct terroir that creates wines with remarkable character.

Adventure Beckons

Slovakia is a veritable gold mine for those with an adventurous spirit. With routes that lead to stunning panoramas and glistening lakes, the High Tatras are a hiker's paradise. These mountains become a white wonderland in the winter, beckoning skiers and snowboarders to glide down immaculate slopes.

Enthusiasts of caving will be lured to the complex networks of caverns, which include the well-known Domica Cave and other underground wonders just waiting to be discovered. If unwinding is your goal, treat yourself to a healing experience in one of the nation's many thermal springs.

Warmth and Hospitality

Beyond its scenic beauty and cultural gems, Slovakia's real asset is the kindness of its people. You will feel accepted as a member of the community and not merely welcomed thanks to the Slovaks' warm hospitality. Talk to people, tell tales over a cup of kofola (a popular soft drink in Slovakia), and let Slovakia permeate your spirit.

Open your heart to the wonder that awaits you in Slovakia as you set out on this adventure. Every minute of your Slovakian adventure, whether it be exploring medieval towns, climbing mountain summits, or simply enjoying the pleasures of the cuisine, will be a brushstroke in the painting that is your trip.

Conclusion: Your Slovakian Odyssey Begins

Welcome to Slovakia, where the past and present coexist, the beauty of nature is shown, and each moment offers the chance to create lifelong memories. It's about to become your voyage through the center of Europe's buried treasure. Accept the magic, relish the moments, and allow Slovakia to enthrall you in a manner that only a place with such a wealth of natural beauty and history could. The journey of 2024 commences now.

Geographical Location of Slovakia

Slovakia is a landlocked nation in the heart of Europe. Here are some important Slovakian geographic details:

Locations:

Latitude: about 48.6690° North

Longitude: about 19.6990° Eastern

Bordering Nations:

Germany to the west

Northwest is the Czech Republic

To the north, Poland

Eastern Ukraine

Hungary's southern region

Terrain Area:

The total area of Slovakia is approximately 49,037 square kilometers (18,933 square miles).

The topography

Slovakia is known for its varied topography, which includes valleys, lowlands, and mountains.

The country's northern and central regions are dominated by the Carpathian Mountains, of which the High Tatras is the tallest mountain range.

The rich Danube River valley and lowlands make up the southern areas.

Creeks:

The Danube River is a significant watercourse that passes through Slovakia's southwest.

The Váh, Hron, and Ipel are a few other important rivers.

Natural Attributes:

Slovakia is home to several stunning natural areas, national parks like the High Tatras National Park, and cave systems like the Demanovska Cave system.

Major Cities and the Capital:

Bratislava, the capital city of Slovakia, is located on the Danube River.

A few other significant cities are Banská Bystrica, Žilina, and Košice.

Weather:

Slovakia has distinct seasons and a temperate continental climate.

Summers are usually mild, while winters can be chilly with snowfall in the mountainous areas.

Knowing Slovakia's geographic setting helps one appreciate its varied landscape, which adds to the attraction of the nation for travelers interested in both the outdoors and culture.

How to use this manual

Welcome to Slovakia Travel Guide: Crafting Memories in the Heart of Europe- Your 2024 Journey Begins

Congratulations on selecting this all-inclusive travel guide to help you discover Slovakia's natural beauty, rich cultural heritage, and exciting adventures in 2024. To guarantee that you get the most out of your trip through the center of Europe, this guide has been painstakingly created. Here's how to use this guidebook to its fullest potential:

1. Getting Started

Introduction

To learn more about the essence of the Slovakian experience, read the introduction.

. What Is Special About Slovakia?

Explore the salient features of Slovakia that will pique your interest and send you on a journey.

. Making Travel Plans:

Recognize the practical parts of travel planning, such as when to visit and what essentials to pack.

2. The Cultural Tapestry

2.1 Historical Highlights:

Explore Slovakia's historical and cultural sites to learn more about the country's rich past.

Folk Traditions and Festivals:

Discover the colorful customs and celebrations that characterize Slovakia's cultural calendar.

2.3 Architectural Marvels:

Discover the architectural treasures that depict Slovakia's development over time.

2.4 Galleries and Museums:

Take in Slovakia's rich artistic and historical legacy by visiting its many museums and galleries.

3.Cityscape Exploration

3.1 Capital Charms: Bratislava

Discover the hidden gems of Slovakia's capital city, including its modern attractions and historical sites.

3.2 Košice: Oriental Style:

Discover Košice's distinct appeal by immersing yourself in its artistic and cultural attractions.

3.3 Banská Bystrica: History of Mining:
Explore Banská Bystrica's cultural riches and industrial legacy.

3.4 Trnava—The Dimly Named Rome
Discover the religious and historical significance of Trnava, often known as "The Little Rome."

4. Nature's Symphony

4.1 Peaks and Trails in the High Tatras:
Arrange your mountain journey, discovering the High Tatras' peaks and hiking paths.

4.2 National Park of Slovak Paradise:
Savor the splendors of Slovak Paradise National Park's natural surroundings.

4.3 Danube River: Magnificent Watercourses:
Discover the breathtaking scenery along the Danube River's banks as you follow its journey.

4.4 Pieniny National Park: Beyond the Rafting Area:
Take a trip to Pieniny National Park, which is well-known for its beautiful scenery and rafting options.

5. Adventure Awaits

5.1 Nature Hikes and Trails:
Arrange your hiking adventures in Slovakia's many landscapes.

5.2 Tatra Mountains Skiing:

Experience the Tatras' wintry paradise by engaging in skiing and snowboarding.

5.3 Exploration and Caving:

Discover Slovakia's hidden treasures by exploring its enthralling caves.

5.4 Health Benefits of Thermal Springs:

Take a moment to unwind and revitalize yourself in Slovakia's healing thermal springs.

6. Culinary Delights

6.1 Customary Slovak Food:

Savor the tastes of traditional Slovak cuisine to the fullest.

6.2 Dishes You Must Try:

Discover the dishes that best capture the essence of Slovak cuisine.

6.3 Regional Markets and Culinary Adventures:

Visit markets and sample real cuisine to immerse yourself in the local culinary scene.

6.4 Spirits and Wine:

Learn about the distinctive wines and spirits that Slovakia's abundant viticulture has to offer.

7. Unique Experiences

7.1 Tours of Medieval Castles:

Take guided tours of Slovakia's numerous medieval castles to travel back in time.

7.2 Conventional Crafts:

Engage with regional artists and discover the artistry of traditional Slovak handicrafts.

7.3 Stays in Villages:

Experience the allure of Slovak villages by staying in real villages.

7.4 Regional Celebrations and Events:

To fully capture the essence of Slovakia, schedule your vacation around regional celebrations and festivals.

8. Practical Travel Tips

8.1 A Guide to Transportation:

Discover the best ways to get across Slovakia by using our information on available transit.

8.2 Lodging Selections:

Select the ideal lodging option based on your preferences and financial constraints.

8.3 Banking and Currency:

Learn useful advice about handling your money while you're visiting.

8.4 Spoken Word and Listening:

Acquire a basic command of Slovak and comprehend the subtleties of local communication.

9. Responsible Travel

9.1 Ecologically Friendly Projects:

Investigate eco-friendly travel strategies to reduce your impact on the environment.

9.2 Etiquette and Cultural Respect:

Recognize and accept the regional etiquette and customs to enrich your cultural experience.

9.3 Encouragement of Local Communities:

Find methods to make a constructive contribution to the communities you visit.

10 Your Slovakian Itinerary

10.1 A Well-Balanced Week in Slovakia:

Create a one-week schedule that gives visitors a well-rounded overview of Slovakia.

10.2 Extensive Investigation: A Two-Week Journey:

Take a two-week itinerary to extend your trip and give yourself more time for a thorough investigation.

10.3 Personalizing Your Visit:

Plan your schedule according to your hobbies and personal preferences.

11. Beyond Slovakia

11.1 Local Points of Interest:

For a longer trip across Europe, check out the sights in nearby nations.

11.2 Associated Nations:

Recognize the easy travel links Slovakia has with its surrounding countries.

11.3 Traveling Through Central Europe:

Think about taking a closer look at Central Europe and its many cultures.

Best Time to Visit Slovakia

Depending on your interests and the kind of experience you're looking for, there is no set optimal time to visit Slovakia. Slovakia has a year-round variety of sights and activities due to its temperate continental environment with distinct seasons. To assist you in choosing when to schedule your visit, the seasons are broken down as follows:

1. Spring: April to June

Weather: Springtime brings with it a surge of greenery, flowering landscapes, and milder temperatures.

Highlights:

. Perfect for outdoor pursuits like hiking and national park exploration.

. Take in the sight of blooming flowers and sprouting trees as nature awakens.

. Nice weather for touring the city and engaging in cultural events.

2. Summertime: July to August

Weather: The weather is warm to hot, marking the height of the travel season.

Highlights:

. Ideal for outdoor activities like hiking and swimming.

. During the summer, festivals and activities are in full swing.

. Longer days afford additional time for sightseeing and exploring.

3. Autumn: September to November

Weather: brisk, chilly air accompanied by vibrant fall foliage.

Highlights:

. Beautiful autumn scenery in the mountains, particularly in the High Tatras.

. As in the summer, hiking and other outdoor activities are still popular, although with fewer people.

. In the wine regions, grape harvest season is a pleasure for wine connoisseurs.

4. Winter: January to February

Weather: chilly temperatures and snowfall, particularly in the highlands.

Highlights:

. Excellent skiing and snowboarding conditions make it the perfect destination for winter sports aficionados.

. Wonderful Christmas markets in Košice and Bratislava.

. Thermal springs offer a warm haven from the bitter cold of winter.

Consideration

Tourist Crowds: June through August is the busiest travel season, thus popular attractions may see heavier crowds during this time. There are less tourists and a more laid-back vibe in the spring and autumn.

Outdoor Activities: Late spring to early autumn is the best time to go hiking, trekking, and on outdoor excursions. For those who enjoy skiing and other winter sports, winter is perfect.

Cultural Events: See if there are any festivals, celebrations, or other events on the local calendar that would be of interest to you. Summer is a busy season for cultural events.

In summary:

In the end, your choices and the experiences you want to have will determine when is the best time to visit Slovakia. Slovakia offers lots to offer all year round, whether you're more interested in the brilliant foliage of autumn, the flowering landscapes of spring, the outdoor experiences of summer, or the winter wonderland for skiing. To get the most out of your trip to this captivating European location, think about the pursuits you wish to engage in and the ambiance you like.

What Makes Slovakia Unique

Slovakia is a charming, individual country that is tucked away in the heart of Europe. Its experience is distinct from other travel locations due to a confluence of historical, cultural, and environmental elements. These are some of the main characteristic

1. Rich Historical Tapestry:

Medieval Castles: Slovakia is home to a remarkable collection of medieval fortifications and castles, each with a distinct architectural style and history. These ancient sites, which include the recognizable Spiš Castle and the fanciful Orava Castle, transport tourists back in time.

Cultural Heritage: The cities, towns, and villages around the nation are intricately linked to its past. The capital, Bratislava, features a fusion of Gothic, Baroque, and Medieval styles. Slovakia's cultural diversity is further enhanced by Košice, which boasts a well-preserved old town, and Banská Štiavnica, a UNESCO World Heritage site.

2. Diverse Natural Beauty

High Tatras: The stunning alpine vistas may be found in the High Tatras mountain range, which is a part of the Carpathians. This area draws both nature lovers and thrill seekers with its craggy peaks, glistening lakes, and picturesque hiking paths.

Caverns and Karst Formations: Slovakia is home to a large number of caverns, notably the Slovak Karst and Aggtelek Karst Caves, which are classified by UNESCO. The stalactite and stalagmite-adorned underground wonders lend an enigmatic and alluring quality to the nation's natural attractions.

3. Cultural Fusion:

Crossroads of Culture: Slovakia, which is located at the meeting point of Central and Eastern Europe, has been influenced by many different cultures. Its past has been molded by influences from Poland, Czech, Austria, and Hungary, resulting in a distinct cultural mosaic that is evident in its customs, folklore, and food.

Festivals and Traditions: The vibrant Červený Kameň Castle Celebrations and the UNESCO-listed fujara and valaška music traditions are just two examples of the vibrant Slovak festivals that offer a glimpse into the nation's diverse cultural heritage.

4. Warm Hospitality:

Slovakian Hospitality: Guests are left with a deep impression of the Slovak people's warmth and friendliness. The true warmth and inviting spirit of the Slovak people add to the distinctive character of the country, whether you're strolling through a scenic town or mingling with locals in the city.

5. Culinary Delights:

Traditional Cuisine: Slovak food reflects the agricultural roots of the nation and is a delightful blend of robust flavors. Taste traditional Slovak cuisine with dishes like kapustnica (cabbage soup) and bryndzové halušky (potato dumplings with sheep cheese).

Local Products: Tokaj and the Small Carpathians, two of Slovakia's wine areas, produce excellent wines. In addition, guests can enjoy locally produced pastries, cheeses, and alcoholic beverages, which enhances the culinary experience.

6. Adorable villages and pristine landscapes:

Picturesque Villages: Slovakia is home to several quaint, attractive villages that lie outside of its cities. The agricultural beauty of the country is best shown in Vlkolínec, a UNESCO-listed village with a well-preserved medieval wooden building.

Untouched Nature: Slovakia's national parks and protected areas demonstrate the country's dedication to environmental preservation. Unspoiled vistas, spotless lakes, and thick forests provide a haven in the arms of nature.

In Summary:

Slovakia's distinctive quality is its ability to combine a rich historical legacy with a variety of stunning natural settings, cultural fusion, friendly hospitality, and a cuisine that captures the spirit of the country. Slovakia invites travelers to explore the undiscovered jewel in the center of Europe, offering an experience that is both unique and unforgettable, whether you're touring historic castles, hiking in the High Tatras, or enjoying regional cuisine.

Planning Your Journey

The first step in guaranteeing a hassle-free and delightful trip to Slovakia is organizing your travel itinerary. Here's a thorough guide to help you plan your unforgettable trip to this alluring European destination, from knowing when to visit to making practical plans.

1. Selecting the Appropriate Time to Go:
. Think about the seasons: Slovakia has a distinct experience for every season. While summer draws people with its festivities and verdant scenery, spring and autumn are better for outdoor activities and pleasant weather. For those who enjoy skiing and other winter sports, winter is ideal.

2. Budgeting for Travel:
. Make a reasonable budget for your vacation, taking into account lodging, transportation, food, entertainment, and other small costs.

. Currency exchange: Learn about the current exchange rates and become familiar with the local currency, which is the euro.

3. How to Get There:

. Travel: Look into and reserve flights well in advance to get the greatest deals. Two important airports are Košice International Airport and Bratislava Airport.

. Transportation inside Slovakia: Arrange your domestic travel, whether it be by bus, train, or rental automobile.

4. Accommodation:

. Look into your lodging alternatives; Slovakia has a variety of places to stay, from opulent hotels to quaint guesthouses. Depending on your preferences and financial constraints, research and reserve lodging.

. Think about location: Depending on your travel schedule, pick lodging that is either ideally situated or conveniently accessible.

5. Recognizing Regional Culture:

. While English is widely spoken in tourist regions, becoming conversant in a few simple Slovak words will enrich your cultural experience.

. Cultural etiquette: To honor Slovak cultures and traditions, familiarize yourself with local conventions and etiquette.

6. Making a Schedule:

. Decide which places are a must-see: Make a list of the main sights and places you wish to see based on your interests.

. Plan your activities: List the things you want to do each day, taking into account the season and the special attractions in each area.

7. Packaging Requirements:

. Weather-appropriate attire: Bring clothes that are suited for the time of year you will be visiting, such as summertime light layers or wintertime warm layers.

. Comfortable footwear: Slovakia's varied terrain may call for a variety of shoe styles, from casual walking shoes to robust hiking boots.

. Essential travel things include passports, adapters, chargers, and any other items that may be needed for the activities you have scheduled.

8. Insurance for Travel:

. Invest in comprehensive travel insurance to protect you against unforeseen disruptions, medical emergencies, and other problems.

9. Health-Guard Measures:

. Verify the vaccination requirements. Take into account any essential immunizations or safety precautions based on the season and your health.

. Keep any prescription drugs you may need with you, along with a basic first aid kit.

10. Connecting with Locals:

. Embark on guided tours, cooking lessons, or cultural excursions to make new friends and expand your travel experience with the locals.

. Ask for advice: Don't be afraid to ask locals for advice about off-the-beaten-path sights, genuine restaurants, and hidden gems.

11. Emergency Details:

. Keep crucial numbers handy: Make a list of emergency contacts, including the number of the closest embassy or consulate and the local authorities.

. Learn about the emergency protocols in your area.

12. Staying Informed:

. Keep up with travel advisories: Before and throughout your journey, look for any updates or travel advisories about your destination.

. Keep connected: To ensure a seamless travel experience, have access to a trustworthy information source, like a smartphone or travel app.

By thoroughly organizing your trip to Slovakia, taking into account things like the ideal time to go, your spending limit, your lodging options, and cultural considerations, you'll create the conditions for a smooth and enjoyable trip.

Accept Slovakia's distinct appeal as you discover its historical sites, breathtaking natural features, and rich cultural heritage.

2. The Cultural Tapestry

Historical Highlights

Slovakia has a rich and varied past that has greatly influenced its identity, architecture, and culture. Discovering Slovakia's historical sites transports you through centuries of development shaped by the influences of many civilizations. The following significant historical moments encapsulate the spirit of Slovakia's past:

1. Romans and Celts:

Prehistoric Settlements: There is proof that people have lived in the area since the Palaeolithic period.

Celtic Influence: Before the Romans arrived, the Celts lived in the region and left behind cultural remnants.

2. The Great Moravian Empire (9th-10th Century):

First Independent Slavic State: The Great Moravian Empire was the first independent Slavic state and was crucial to the political and cultural advancement of the Slavic people.

Cyril and Methodius: Their arrival brought with them the Cyrillic script and the Glagolitic alphabet, which had a profound impact on the region's religious and cultural milieu.

3. Kingdom of Hungary (11th–19th century):

Kingdom of Hungary: Centuries of Hungarian influence resulted in Slovakia joining the Kingdom of Hungary.

Turkish Ottoman Wars: The Ottoman Empire's growth presented Slovakia with difficulties, and battles and conflicts left their mark on the region.

4. The Habsburg Monarchy (16th-19th Century):

Habsburg Rule: Slovakia joined the Habsburg Monarchy, which enhanced the area's heterogeneous makeup.

Reformation and Counter-Reformation: Slovakia's religious variety was influenced by the Protestant Reformation and the Counter-Reformation that followed.

5. Austro-Hungarian Empire (19th Century): Industrialization: With the expansion of manufacturing, transportation, and mining infrastructure, the 19th century saw a major industrial development.

National Revival: With a focus on Slovak identity and language, a phase of cultural and national revival developed.

6. Czechoslovakia (20th Century):

Formation of Czechoslovakia: Following World War I, Czechs and Slovaks united to form Czechoslovakia.

World War II: Following the Slovak National Uprising against the Nazis in 1944, Slovakia emerged as a distinct state under Nazi rule.

Communist Era: Slovakia joined the Eastern Bloc after World War II and was ruled by communists there until the Velvet Revolution in 1989.

7. Independence (1993- Present):

Czechoslovakia's dissolution: On January 1, 1993, the country peacefully broke up into the Czech Republic and Slovakia.

Integration with the EU: Slovakia's 2004 entry into the EU was a major turning point in its post-communist growth.

8. Historical Sites:

Spiš Castle: One of the biggest castle complexes in Europe, Spiš Castle is a UNESCO World Heritage site that provides breathtaking views and an insight into medieval history.

Bratislava Castle: Situated above the capital, Bratislava Castle has been significant to Slovakia's past and is a representation of the tenacity of the people.

Banská Štiavnica: Slovakia's mining tradition is reflected in the well-preserved medieval mining building of Banská Štiavnica, a town designated by UNESCO.

Červený Kameň Castle: Distinguished by its Renaissance design, this castle has functioned as a fortification and a dwelling over the years.

A thorough grasp of Slovakia's journey through many eras, identity formation, and contribution to the distinctive cultural fabric that distinguishes the nation today can be gained by investigating its historical highlights.

Folk Traditions and Festivals

Slovakia's unique cultural past is reflected in its complex tapestry of folk traditions and festivals. These festivities, which have their roots in centuries-old rituals, highlight the richness and vibrancy of Slovak traditions. Take in the vibrant world of folklore while discovering some of Slovakia's most important customs and celebrations:

1. Festival of Folklore Východná:

Location: Východná

Time: June's end

Highlights:

Among Slovakia's biggest and most well-known folklore events.

Features traditional crafts, dance, and music from around the world.

Captivating performances by folklore groups with vibrant choreography and real costumes.

2. Days of Folk Culture (Krasnohorské Dni Čudovej Kultúry):

Location: Podhradie Krasnohorská

Time: July

Highlights:

Honors the folklore of Hungary and Slovakia.

To display their abilities, craftspeople, artists, and folk ensembles come together.

Performances of traditional music and dance take audiences deep into the heart of Slovak folklore.

3. Fašiangy (Shrovetide):

Time: January–February

Highlights:

A holiday held before Lent that is marked by vibrant processions.

The Festive masks, traditional clothes, and music define the processions of Fašiangy.

The "burial of the double bass" marks the end of winter in some areas.

4. Noci Svatého Jána (Midsummer Night):

Time: June 23-24

Highlights:

Combines dancing, music, and bonfires to commemorate the summer solstice.

Folk rituals are carried out to drive out bad spirits and promote wealth.

Jumping over bonfires is a traditional behavior associated with good health and luck.

5. Folk Festival Detva:

Location: Detva

Time: July

Highlights:

Committed to protecting and advancing Slovak traditional folk culture.

Includes displays of crafts and performances of folk music and dancing.

A venue for presenting localized folklore from Slovakia.

6. Záhorácke Dancing, or Záhorácke Čardáše:

Location: The Záhorie region

Time:August

Highlights:

Honors the Záhorie region's folk dancing customs.

Bright costumes, traditional dances, and music take center stage.

Enthusiastic involvement from both locals and tourists.

7. Festival of Krakovany Plums:

Location: Krakovany

Time: August
Highlights:
Celebrates the plum harvest by serving traditional food, music, and dance.
Offers plum brandy samples, plum-themed competitions, and a festive setting.
A celebration of regional food traditions and agriculture.

8. Kosovo Day:
Location: Košice
Time: 7 May
Highlights:
Honors Saint Elisabeth of Hungary, the patron saint of the city.
Includes folk dance performances, concerts, and a vibrant procession.
Demonstrates the communal spirit and cultural legacy of Košice.

9. Štefánikovo Leto (Summer of Štefánik):
Location: Brezová pod Bradlom.
Time: August
Highlights:
Honors the life and accomplishments of renowned Slovak astronomer and diplomat Milan Rastislav Štefánik.
To commemorate Štefánik's legacy, exhibitions, concerts, and cultural activities are planned.

The celebrations combine folk traditions, providing a fusion of culture and history.

10. Old Times in Komárno / Staré Časy v Komárne

Location: Komárno

Time: August

Highlights:

Makes historical settings come to life through period attire, music, and reenactments.

Includes jousting competitions, medieval games, and traditional crafts.

A trip through time to discover Komárno's rich cultural legacy.

Slovakia's folk customs and celebrations offer an enthralling window into the essence of its culture. With vibrant processions, energetic dance performances, and customary ceremonies, these festivities provide an all-encompassing experience that immerses guests in the core of Slovak folklore. Slovakia's rich cultural past is bound to make an impression, whether you're experiencing it at a big event or learning about local customs while traveling.

Architectural Marvels

Slovakia is home to a diverse range of architectural landmarks, including Baroque churches, modern buildings, and ancient castles. Discovering Slovakia's architectural wonders provides an engrossing historical trip and highlights the variety of influences that have molded the nation's built environment. The following architectural treasures are examples of the country's rich cultural and historical heritage:

1. Castle Spiš:

Location: Šišské Podhradie

Styles: Gothic and Romanesque

Highlights:

One of Central Europe's biggest castle complexes.

A World Heritage Site recognized by UNESCO.

commands the terrain with its commanding presence and expansive vistas.

2. Budapest Castle:

Location: Bratislava

Style:Gothic and Baroque styles

Highlights:

Views the nation's capital from Castle Hill.

Houses the Slovak National Museum and offers historical insights into the nation.

A representation of the tenacity and cultural importance of Bratislava.

3. The Cathedral of Saint Martin:
Location: Bratislava
 Style: Gothic
Highlights:
Hungary's coronation church for monarchs and queens.
Contains the tombs of notable dignitaries and monarchs.
Imposing a building with a lofty spire that dominates the skyline.

4. Town Castle in Banská Bystrica:
Location: Banská Bystrica.
Style:Renaissance
Highlights:
Keeps the town castle's Renaissance architecture intact.
Display about the history and culture of the area.
offers expansive vistas of Banská Bystrica.

5. The Carpathian Mountains' Wooden Churches:
Locations: Hervartov, Tvrdošín, and Kežmarok, among others
Style: Gothic Revival Wooden Structures
Highlights:
Sites listed as World Heritage by UNESCO.
Exemplify elaborately decorated, traditional wooden church architecture.

Represent the local populations' cultural and religious identities.

6. Crown of Bojnice:

Location: Bojnice

Style: Romantic and Neo-Gothic

Highlights:

A lovely palace straight out of a fairy tale.

Organizes the International Festival of Ghosts and Spirits, among other cultural activities.

Gorgeously designed gardens in a lovely location.

7.Saint Elisabeth Cathedral

Location: Košice

Style: Gothic

Highlights:

Slovakia's largest church.

Contains priceless items of art and the Košice Golden Treasure.

An important landmark in the historic core of Košice.

8. Castle Orava:

Location: Oravský Podzámok.

Styles: Renaissance and Gothic

Highlights:

Perched over the Orava River on a tall rock.

A lovely medieval castle that has been kept in good condition.

Used as a setting for multiple film shoots.

9. The Devin Castle

Location: Devin (near Bratislava)

Style:Medieval

Highlights:

Strategically situated where the Danube and Morava rivers converge.

Provides expansive vistas of the surroundings.

Historical relevance for an archaeological site.

10. Church of the Virgin Mary's Assumption:

Location: Teplice Rajecké

Style: Baroque

Highlights:

Recognized for its distinct oval form.

Keeps priceless Baroque artworks.

A portion of Rajecké Teplice, a historic spa town.

Slovakia's remarkable architectural works demonstrate the country's adaptability, cultural diversity, and historical development. Whether touring Gothic cathedrals, Renaissance mansions, or quaint wooden churches, every architectural treasure adds a unique tale to the rich tapestry of Slovakia's cultural past. These buildings are not only stunning to look at, but they also shed light on the past of the nation and the individuals who have influenced its history.

Galleries and Museums

Slovakia has a wide range of museums and galleries that provide extensive insights into the history, art, culture, and scientific accomplishments of the nation. These cultural organizations offer tourists engaging experiences, ranging from interactive exhibitions to world-class art collections. Here are a few notable galleries and museums in Slovakia:

1. National Museum of Slovakia:

Locations: several branches in Bratislava

Highlights:

Consists of multiple divisions, such as the Museum of Jewish Culture and the Historical Museum.

Displays encompassing the history, archaeology, ethnography, and other fields of the nation.

An entry point into the rich cultural legacy of Slovakia.

2. Meulensteen Art Museum in Danubia:

Location: close to Bratislava, in Čunovo

Highlights:

Situated on the Danube River peninsula is a museum dedicated to modern art.

Includes exhibitions of modern Slovak and foreign art.

A distinctive architectural area with breathtaking river views.

3. National Gallery of Slovakia:
Locations: several branches in Bratislava

Highlights:

Contains a vast collection of Slovak artwork spanning the Middle Ages to now.

Paintings, sculptures, decorative arts, and modern works are all on display.

One noteworthy architectural jewel is the branch of Esterházy Palace.

4. The Transport Museum:
Location: Bratislava

Highlights

Displays the development of Slovakia's transportation system.

Displays antique automobiles, trains, planes, and other forms of transportation.

With interactive displays for all age groups, it's suitable for families.

5. Gallery of East Slovakia:
Location: Košice

Highlights:

Focuses on visual arts and has a wide selection of both foreign and Slovak artwork.

Paintings, sculptures, and installations of contemporary art are all on display.

contributes significantly to the development of Eastern Slovakia's cultural landscape.

6. Jewish Cultural Museum:

Location: Bratislava

Highlights:

A section of the Slovak National Museum is Devoted to the conservation of Jewish cultural legacy.

Displays highlighting the history, customs, and contributions of Jews to Slovak culture.

Found within the Zsigray Synagogue.

7. Fulla Gallery Čudovít:

Location: Ružomberok

Highlights:

Devoted to the paintings of well-known Slovak painter Ľudovít Fulla.

Holds a collection of graphic art, paintings, and drawings by Fulla.

The gallery structure is a work of architectural beauty.

8. The Museum of Toys and Puppet Cultures:

Location: Modrý Kameň

Highlights:

Examines Slovakia's puppetry's cultural relevance and history.

Showcases a wide selection of toys, marionettes, and puppets.

Exhibitions that are interesting to both adults and children.

9. Museum of Slovak Mining:

Location: Štiavnica, Banská

Highlights:

Chronicles Slovakia's mining heritage, with a focus on the Banská Štiavnica district.

Displays models of mines, mining equipment, and tools.

Provides tours of historic mining locations underground.

10. Museum of Commerce:

Location: Bratislava

Highlights:

Examines Slovakia's trade and economic history.

Displays highlight how advertising, retail, and consumer culture have changed over time.

Situated inside the historic town hall.

Slovakia's galleries and museums offer a comprehensive look into the cultural, artistic, and historical aspects of the nation. For those who want to learn more about Slovakia's cultural legacy, these institutions provide a wide range of experiences, regardless of their interest in modern art, historical items, or interactive displays.

3. Cityscape Exploration

Bratislava: Capital Charms

Slovakia's capital city, Bratislava, is rich in architectural treasures, rich in history, and home to a thriving arts and culture community. Bratislava, which is tucked away along the Danube River, exudes attractiveness through a harmonious fusion of modern energy, imperial majesty, and medieval beauty. The following are the capital's attractions that draw travelers to Bratislava:

1. The Staré Mesto Old Town:

Cobblestone lanes: Explore the Old Town's winding, narrow lanes, which are dotted with vibrant architecture and quaint eateries.

Michael's Gate: The sole surviving medieval gate in Bratislava, Michael's Gate is a famous entryway into the city.

2. Castle Bratislava (Bratislavský hrad):

Dominant Silhouette: The Bratislava Castle, perched atop Castle Hill, provides sweeping views of the city and the Danube River.

Historical Significance: Discover the history of the castle by visiting exhibitions on

Slovak art, history, and the development of the castle itself.

3. St. Martin Cathedral (Katedrála svätého Martina):

Gothic splendor: Take in St. Martin's Cathedral's stunning Gothic design, which serves as the **Coronation Regalia:** coronation cathedral for Hungarian kings and queens.

Discover the cathedral's function in regal coronations and have a look at the relic of St. Stephen's crown.

4. Most SNP Bridge SNP:

UFO Observation Deck: Reach the top of the SNP Bridge's UFO-shaped tower for expansive views over Bratislava and the surrounding area.

Unusual Design: The UFO Tower gives the landscape of Bratislava a futuristic feel and is a recognizable landmark in the skyline.

5. Palace of Primatials (Primaciálny palác):

Mirror Hall: Admire the magnificent Mirror Hall, where, following the Battle of Austerlitz in 1805, the Pressburg Peace was signed.

English Park: Explore the neighboring English Park, a tranquil haven smack dab in the middle of the metropolis.

6. The Modern Church (Blue Church):

Art Nouveau Marvel: Take a look at the magnificent Blue Church, an example of Art Nouveau design distinguished by its blue hue and ornate details.

Spiritual Ambience: Enter to take in this special place of worship's calm, spiritual atmosphere.

7. The Palace of Grassalkovich (Grassalkovichov palác):

Presidential Mansion: Take in the splendor of Slovakia's official presidential mansion, Grassalkovich Palace.

Presidential Gardens: Unwind in the exquisitely designed gardens that encircle the palace.

8. Slovenské národné divadlo, or the Slovak National Theatre:

Cultural Hub: Take in a show at the Slovak National Theatre, a long-standing theater, opera, and ballet company.

Historic edifice: Situated along the Danube banks, the Neo-Renaissance edifice is a work of art in and of itself.

9. Nový most and Námestie Ľudovíta Štúra/UFO Bridge and Park:

Views of the Riverfront: Take a stroll along the Danube River and enjoy the views of the city skyline and the UFO Bridge.

Fountain of Union: Discover Námestie Čudovíta Štúra, home to the Fountain of Union a representation of the shared past shared by Slovaks and Czechs.

10. Savoury Treats:

Street Food Markets: Sample Slovak and foreign cuisine at the Old Market Hall and other street food markets in Bratislava.

Traditional Restaurants: In the Old Town's quaint traditional restaurants, savor the flavors of Slovak cuisine.

The allure of Slovakia's capital is its ability to eloquently combine the ancient with the modern, providing an engrossing trip through time and culture. Wander around Bratislava's unique charms, from medieval streets to modern perspectives, from ancient castles to modern art scenes, and experience the unique energy of Slovakia's dynamic capital.

Košice: Eastern Elegance

The second-biggest city in Slovakia, Košice, captivates tourists with its unique Eastern European grandeur. Košice beckons exploration with its dynamic cultural scene, a blend of architectural styles, and rich history. The following components add to Košice's Eastern elegance:

1. The Cathedral of Saint Elisabeth (Dóm svätej Alžbety):

Gothic Masterpiece: Take in the splendor of Slovakia's largest Gothic cathedral, St. Elisabeth Cathedral.

Double Spire: One of Košice's most recognizable skyline features is the cathedral's double spire.

2. Main Road, or Hlavná Ulica:

Historical Ambiance: Walk along Main Street, which is dotted with vibrant buildings, quaint eateries, and historical sites, to experience the historical ambiance.

Imperial Architecture: Admire the variety of architectural styles seen in imperial architecture, including Gothic, Baroque, and Renaissance.

3. Štátne divadlo Košice, or the State Theatre of Košice:

Cultural Hub: Take in performances of ballet, opera, and theater at the Košice State Theatre.

Historic Setting: The Neo-Baroque theater gives a refined touch to the local arts scene.

4. Hrajúca Fontána, or Singing Fountain:

Attraction in the City Center: Get together at the Singing Fountain to witness a captivating display of water and light.

Public Events and Gatherings: The fountain frequently acts as the center of attention for these kinds of occasions.

5. Prison Mikluš (Miklušova väznica):

Medieval History: Discover the history of Mikluš Prison, a medieval infirmary featuring conserved cells and historical displays.

City Legends: Discover the urban myths and stories connected to this historical location.

6. Gold Treasure of Košice (Zlatý poklad):

Historical Artifacts: View the Košice Gold Treasure, an assortment of medieval goldsmith creations, at the East Slovak Museum.

Cultural Heritage: The treasure is a testament to the historical and cultural importance of the city.

7. Košice detská železnica, often known as the Children's Railway:

Family-Friendly Attraction: Enjoy a ride on the Košice Children's Railway, a narrow-gauge railroad run by kids under adult supervision, for a family-friendly attraction.

Scenic Route: The beautiful path is a unique experience for tourists of all ages, providing picturesque views of Košice's environs.

8. Gallery Východoslovenská (East Slovak Gallery):

Artistic Exploration: Dive into the vast array of visual arts, from classical to contemporary, that are housed in the East Slovak Gallery.

Local and foreign Art: By presenting exhibitions of both local and foreign artists, the gallery enhances Košice's cultural life.

9. The Iron Arena (Old Ostrow):

Modern Architecture: Take a look at the Steel Arena's spectacular front, which showcases modern ice hockey architecture.

Sports and Entertainment: Košice's lively environment is enhanced by the venue's hosting of a variety of events, such as concerts and sporting contests.

10. Craftsmen Lane (ulička Remeselnícka):

Artisan Quarter: Discover the charming Craftsmen Lane in the Artisan Quarter, where regional craftsmen display their age-old creations.

Handmade Creations: Take a look at handcrafted goods, mementos, and artwork that capture the creative spirit of the city.

The Eastern elegance of Košice is a beautiful fusion of rich cultural diversity, historical grandeur, and a contemporary, energetic atmosphere. Discovering the unique beauty of Košice, an artistic gem in Eastern Slovakia, is a must-do experience for anyone visiting the old streets, seeing live performances, or browsing art treasures. The city is a desirable travel destination for people looking for an exquisite and captivating experience because of its ability to gracefully combine its historic legacy with modern dynamism.

Banská Bystrica: Mining Heritage

Situated in the center of Slovakia, Banská Bystrica is a city that takes pride in its mining history. The city is a live reminder of its rich mining heritage, from its mining history dating back to the Middle Ages to its well-maintained architecture. An overview of Banská Bystrica's mining history is provided below:

1. Ancient Mining Village:
Medieval Origins: Gold and copper mining played a significant part in Banská Bystrica's history as a mining town, which dates back to the 13th century.
Investigate the ruins of the medieval mining villages, which served as the homes and workplaces for miners.
2. Slovenské banské múzeum, or the Slovak Mining Museum:

Heritage Preservation: The museum's mission is to conserve and present the mining heritage of the area.

Exhibitions: Take a look at displays of artifacts, mining tools, and equipment that provide a glimpse into the working days of miners.

3. The Štiavnica Mountains:

Natural Beauty: Mining landscapes and charming mining settlements may be seen in the adjacent Štiavnica Highlands.

Cultural Landscape: The landscape, which is a UNESCO World Heritage site, illustrates the symbiotic interaction that exists between humans and the natural world.

4. Town Castle in Banská Bystrica:

Renaissance Architecture: The Renaissance-style Banská Bystrica Town Castle serves as a reminder of the historical significance of the city.

Museum of Central Slovakia: The museum, which has displays of local history and culture, is housed in the castle.

5. District of Central Slovak Mining:

UNESCO Recognition: Banská Bystrica is a part of the Technical Monuments in its vicinity and the Historic Town of Banská Štiavnica, both of which are classified by UNESCO.

Mining Complexes: Discover how the mining industry was shaped by the shafts, galleries, and water management systems found in mining complexes.

6. Memorial of Andrej Kmeš:

Tribute to Mining Engineer: The Andrej Kmeš Memorial pays tribute to the eminent scientist and mining engineer who made a substantial contribution to the growth of mining in the area.

Legacy in teaching: Kmeť's efforts in mining research and teaching have had a long-lasting effect on the industry.

7. Area of the Old Castle:

Historic Quarters: Take a stroll around the Old Castle Area, which is home to quaint squares, winding alleys, and well-maintained medieval buildings.

Miner's Square: Explore Miner's Square, a focal point encircled by historically significant structures and the Church of the Assumption of the Virgin Mary.

8. Andrej Kmeš High School of Woodworking and Forestry:

Educational Tradition: By emphasizing forestry and wood processing studies, the high school carries on the mining tradition.

Architectural Interest: The school's old building is a treasure that embodies the community's educational history.

9. Monuments Mined:

Miner's Statue: See monuments and statues honoring miners for their laborious efforts and contributions to the growth of the city.

Mining Symbols: A variety of public areas and architectural elements incorporate mining symbols, such as pickaxes and hammers.

10. Industrial Past:

Old Mining Machinery: Get a real sense of the city's industrial heritage by visiting outdoor exhibits that feature vintage mining machinery and equipment.

Educational Trails: Explore educational pathways that offer insightful insights into the mining and industrial history of the city.

The mining history of Banská Bystrica is a dynamic story that is ingrained in the city's fabric rather than merely a historical chapter. Banská Bystrica welcomes tourists to explore its mining history and witness the tenacity of a town fashioned by the riches lying beneath its soil, from the well-preserved medieval structures to the educational institutions carrying on the legacy.

Trnava: The Little Rome

Known as "The Little Rome," Trnava is a beautiful city in western Slovakia with a rich history based mostly on its ecclesiastical legacy and stunning architecture. Here's a taste of what makes Trnava an alluring travel destination evoking the splendor of Rome:

1. St. John the Baptist Cathedral of (Dóm svätého Jána Krstiteča):

Spiritual Center: The cathedral serves as Trnava's primary church and a place of spiritual gathering.

Baroque Architecture: Take in the elaborate interior design, which includes beautiful altars and holy artwork.

2. Ancient City Walls:

Fortifications: Trnava has well-preserved bastions and city walls that were formerly part of a defense system.

Ancient Charm: Take a stroll around the walls to take in the expansive vistas and feel the city's ancient charm.

3. Church of Saint Nicholas (Kostol svätého Mikuláša):

Jesuit Legacy: The city's Jesuit tradition is demonstrated by this Jesuit church.

Architectural Magnificence: The church's design exemplifies the Baroque era's grandeur.

4. College Jesuit (Jezuitská kolej):

Educational Legacy: Investigate the Jesuit College, an establishment that left a lasting impact on culture and education.

Baroque Library: The college's Baroque library is a veritable gold mine of old books and manuscripts.

5. Holy Trinity Square, also known as Námestie svätej Trojice,

Central Square: Encircled by old buildings, Holy Trinity Square is the focal point of Trnava.

Monuments and Fountains: Take in the monuments and fountains that add to the charming atmosphere of the square.

6. Trnava University (Trnavská univerzita):

Academic Heritage: Trnava's dedication to education is reflected in the university, which was established in 1635.

Historic Structures: There are several historically significant buildings on campus.

7. Rennesančná radničná veža, also known as Renaissance Town Tower:

Famous Tower: One of the most noticeable structures in Trnava's skyline is the Renaissance Town Tower.

Observation Deck: Ascend to the top of the observation deck for sweeping views of the city and its environs.

8. Mestská synagóga, or City Synagogue:

Jewish Heritage: Discover Trnava's historical Jewish community by touring the City Synagogue, a tribute to its Jewish heritage.

Architectural aspects: The synagogue is a cultural center with distinctive architectural aspects.

9. The Palace of the Archbishop (Arcibiskupský palác):

Historical Residency: The archbishops of Esztergom lived in the Archbishop's Palace.

Architectural Significance: The palace's design incorporates several old-world architectural motifs.

10. Parks and Gardens in Cities:

Calm Encounters: Trnava's tranquil parks and gardens offer calm escapes from the bustle of the city.

Scenic Walks: Wander through parks and green areas that enhance the overall appeal of the city on a stroll.

"The Little Rome," Trnava, is a synthesis of architectural genius, spirituality, and rich history. Immerse yourself in the rich cultural tapestry of the city, which unfolds like a living museum with its religious landmarks, ancient squares, and educational institutions. Trnava is a mesmerizing place that echoes the grandeur of Rome on a smaller scale because of its unique fusion of Baroque grace, academic legacy, and spiritual significance.

4. Nature's Symphony

The High Tatras: Peaks and Trails

The breathtaking High Tatras mountain range, which borders Slovakia and Poland, entices hikers with its towering peaks, crystal-clear alpine lakes, and extensive network of picturesque paths. A peek at the peaks and paths that turn the High Tatras into a nature lover's and outdoor enthusiast's paradise is provided here:

1. štít Gerlachovský:

Highest Peak: The highest peak in the Carpathian mountain range and the High Tatras is Gerlachovský štít, rising to a height of 2,655 meters.

Difficult Ascent: Climbing Gerlachovský štít is a difficult journey that rewards climbers with amazing vistas.

2. Czech Pleso:

Alpine Lake: Encircled by the peaks of the High Tatras, Štrbské Pleso is a charming alpine lake.

Hiking Base: Known for its beautiful waters that reflect stunning views of the peaks, this location is a popular starting point for a variety of hiking paths.

3. Rysy

Polish-Slovak Border: Rysy is the highest peak in all of Poland and it crosses the border between Slovakia and Poland.

Routes Less Traveled: Several paths go to Rysy and offer sweeping views of the surroundings.

4. Prague's Pleso:

Mountain Lake: Popradské Pleso is a serene mountain lake that is tucked away at an elevation of 1,494 meters.

Enchanting Setting: Nestled between towering peaks and rich foliage, this place is a calm place to relax.

5. Lomnica Tatranská:

Gateway Town: Tatranská Lomnica is a town that acts as a gateway to the High Tatras and provides access to the well-known cable car that goes to Lomnický štít.

Ski Resort: Tatranská Lomnica opens as a ski resort in the winter, drawing fans of the cold wea

6. Lomnický štít:

Panoramic Views: Lomnický štít, which is accessible by cable car, provides breathtaking views of the neighboring peaks from above.

Observatory: A meteorological station and observatory are located atop the summit.

7. Velická dolina, or Velická Valley:

Alpine Meadow: Encircled by high peaks, Velická Valley is an alpine meadow.

paths and Huts: The valley is crisscrossed by a multitude of paths, and mountain huts offer refuge to hikers.

8. The Hrebienok

Family-Friendly: There are a variety of hiking trails in Hrebienok that are appropriate for hikers of all skill levels.

Waterfalls: Take a hike along one of the neighboring waterfalls, such as the well-known Studenovodské vodopády.

9. KraviĈ:

Symbolic Peak: The Slovakian coat of arms features Kriváň, who is frequently regarded as a symbol of the nation.

Popular Ascent: Renowned for its breathtaking views of the surrounding mountains, the ascent to Kriváň is a popular trip.

10. Voda Biela:

Nature Reserve: Biela Voda is a nature reserve renowned for its wide variety of plants and animals.

Educational paths: This immaculate natural setting is explored by visitors via educational paths.

The paths and peaks of the High Tatras create a tapestry of breathtaking natural beauty that beckons adventure enthusiasts to explore their challenging landscape. The High Tatras provide an immersive experience in the center of Europe's alluring wilderness, whether you choose to climb to the highest peaks, travel through alpine meadows, or simply take in the peace of mountain lakes.

Slovak Paradise National Park

Nestled in the eastern region of Slovakia, the Slovak Paradise National Park is a haven for nature lovers, boasting lush woods, breathtaking gorges, thunderous waterfalls, and an exciting network of hiking paths. A sample of the marvels that characterize Slovak Paradise National Park is provided here:

1. Velická dolina, or Velická Valley:

Beautiful scenery: Those who love the outdoors will find paradise in the Velická Valley, which has immaculate scenery.

Hiking Trails: Hikers can enjoy breathtaking views of the surrounding mountains as trails wind across the valley.

2. Gorge Suchá Belá:

Magnificent Gorge: The Suchá Belá River flows through the spectacular gorge, which is renowned for its glistening pure waters and its high rock cliffs.

Via Ferrata: Climbers can use chains, ladders, and a via ferrata path to get through the gorge.

3. Hornádu Prielom:

Hornád River Gorge: The Hornád River sculpted Prielom Hornádu, a gorge with steep rocks and abundant greenery.

River Crossing: Hiking paths have areas where users can cross rivers using wooden footbridges.

4. Piecky Canyon:

Slender Paths: Piecky Gorge is well-known for its slender paths, wooden boardwalks, and fascinating "rock towns."

Waterfalls: As they tumble down the rocky rocks, waterfalls elicit a mystical ambiance.

5. Pavel Tomasovsky:

Scenery: Tomasovsky Vyhlad provides a broad perspective of the surrounding topography.

Trekking Reward: This viewpoint, which is accessible through trekking routes, is a worthwhile stop for anyone venturing through the park.

6. Dobšinská čadová jaskyňa, also known as Dobšinská Ice Cave:

Natural Wonder: Dobšinská Ice Cave, a UNESCO World Heritage site, is a marvel of nature with distinctive ice formations.

Guided Tours: Take a guided tour through the cave's chambers to see the enthralling ice sculptures.

7. Krisel:

Rock Formations: Kysel is renowned for its striking rock formations, which include organic arches and towers.

Possibilities for Climbing: Climbers can take on the park's granite walls, which provide an air of excitement.

8. Klebrátisko:

Historical Site: The remnants of a Carthusian monastery may be found at Kláštorisko, a historical site.

Hiking Hub: The region is the starting point for several hiking paths that combine the natural world with history.

9. Výhčad Tomášovský:

Viewpoint: Tomášovský Výhčad offers a breathtaking perspective of the Slovak Paradise scenery that surrounds it.

Accessible climb: This viewpoint is well-liked by tourists because it's reachable via a reasonably easy climb.

10. Lúka Meadow Dlhá:

Natural Clearing: Encircled by thick woodlands, Dlhá Lúka is a charming meadow.

Leisure Spot: Amidst the park's natural splendor, it provides a peaceful area for picnics and leisure.

Slovakia's natural landscapes are diverse and breathtakingly beautiful, as demonstrated by the Slovak Paradise National Park. For outdoor enthusiasts and those looking to get in touch with the unspoiled wilderness of Eastern Slovakia, the park provides a variety of experiences, from stunning gorges to tranquil meadows, and from tough via ferrata treks to the charming Dobšinská Ice Cave.

The Danube River: Majestic Waterways

The Danube River, known as the "Queen of Europe's Rivers," is a magnificent river that connects many landscapes, civilizations, and historical periods as it winds through the center of the continent. Here is a taste of some of the captivating sights and activities found along the magnificent Danube River:

1. The Black Forest's source:

Charming Origins: The Danube begins in Germany's Black Forest, which is encircled by lush trees and beautiful scenery.

Investigating the Source: Before the river sets out on its epic voyage, visitors can investigate the source region, designated by a modest spring.

2. Germany's Regensburg:

Historic Cityscape: Regensburg's picturesque medieval cityscape along the Danube is one of the highlights of this UNESCO World Heritage site.

Stone Bridge: The city's two charming riverbanks are connected by the famous Stone Bridge, which spans the river.

3. Region of Wachau, Austria:

Vineyard Landscapes: The Austrian Wachau Valley is well-known for its picturesque villages, terraced vineyards, and historic castles.

Melk Abbey: A cultural treasure along the Danube, Melk Abbey is set on a hill overlooking the river.

4. Hungary's Budapest:

Buda and Pest: The Danube divides Budapest, the capital city of Hungary, into Buda and Pest.

Stunning vistas: Along the river are breathtaking vistas of the city's icons, such as the Parliament Building and Buda Castle.

5. Serbia, Romania, and Iron Gates:

Natural Wonder: The Iron Gates, a ravine that naturally divides Serbia and Romania, is a wonder of nature.

Magnificent Cliffs: Passing through the Iron Gates provides a vista of the Tabula Traiana monument and soaring cliffs.

6. Serbia's Belgrade:

Historic Confluence: Belgrade is a dynamic city with a rich history located where the Danube and Sava rivers converge.

Kalemegdan Fortress: The Kalemegdan Fortress offers sweeping views of the rivers and stands watch over the confluence.

7. Romania's Danube Delta:

Natural Oasis: A maze of marshes, rivers, and wildlife, the Danube Delta is a UNESCO Biosphere Reserve.

Birdwatching Paradise: Birdwatchers can see a wide variety of bird species in this distinctive deltaic ecology, making it a bird watcher's paradise.

8. Slovakia's Bratislava:

Castle on the Hill: Slovakia's capital, Bratislava, is home to a historic castle with a view of the Danube.

Old Town Charm: Wander around the quaint Old Town, where riverbanks are lined with old buildings and cafes.

9. Austria's Vienna:

Imperial Grandeur: Vienna, the capital of Austria, is renowned for its museums, imperial palaces, and legacy of classical music.

Riverside Culture: Savor the lively environment along the Danube Canal, as well as riverfront concerts and cultural activities.

10. Romania's Black Sea Delta:

Danube mouth: The Black Sea Delta, a dynamic and constantly shifting natural habitat, is where the Danube ends.

Unique Biodiversity: For those who love the outdoors, the delta is a home for a wide variety of plants and animals.

Europe's unifying and connecting force, the Danube River winds through a variety of scenic regions and ancient cities. The Danube offers a journey into the center of the continent, providing a tapestry of experiences and cultural richness, whether you cruise along its waterways, discover quaint riverside towns, or marvel at the natural beauty along its banks.

Pieniny National Park: Rafting and Beyond

The gorgeous Pieniny National Park is located in the southern portion of Poland and the northern part of Slovakia. It is well-known for its breathtaking scenery, narrow river gorges, and outdoor activities. One of the most well-liked activities in the park is rafting on the Dunajec River, but there's plenty more to discover. Here's a taste of what awaits visitors in Pieniny National Park activities other than rafting:

1. Rafting the Dunajec River:

Magnificent Gorge: With sheer limestone cliffs on all sides, rafting the Dunajec River through the spectacular Pieniny Gorge is an exciting experience.

Traditional Wooden Rafts: Take on the journey with knowledgeable local experts guiding you on traditional wooden rafts.

2. Three Crowns, or Trzy Korony:

Majestic Summit: With sweeping views of the surrounding landscapes, Trzy Korony is the highest peak in the Pieniny Mountains.

Hiking Trails: Discover hiking paths that ascend to the summit and provide trekkers with breathtaking views as a reward.

3. Homole Canyon:

Natural Beauty: With its unusual rock formations, luxuriant vegetation, and gushing waterfalls, Homole Gorge is a hidden treasure.

Hiking Adventures: Explore the gorge's natural treasures by hiking

4. Sokolica:

Iconic Rock Formation: The limestone formation known as Sokolica provides breathtaking views of the surrounding peaks and the Dunajec River.

Chapel of St. John the Baptist: For a taste of culture, stop by the Chapel of St. John the Baptist, which is situated atop Sokolica.

5. Castle Czorsztyn:

Historic Fortress: Perched on a hill with a panoramic view of the Pieniny Mountains and Lake Czorsztyn, Czorsztyn Castle is a historic fortress.

Cultural exploration: Take in the expansive views from the castle's towers, explore its interiors, and discover its history.

6. Rafting on White Water:

Extreme Excitation: Those looking for an even more exhilarating experience can go white water rafting on specific Dunajec River areas.

Expert Guides: With the help of knowledgeable teachers, raft through difficult rapids.

7. Ski Jaworki Area:

Winter Activities: Skiers and snowboarders congregate in the Jaworki Ski Area during the winter months.

Snow-Covered Landscapes: Enjoy Pieniny National Park's winter scenery during a different time of year.

8. Dunajec Bike Path:

Scenic Ride: A scenic ride along the river is available for cyclists of all ability levels on the Dunajec Cycling Trail.

Nature Exploration: Ride a bike through the park to learn about its plants and animals.

9. The Museum of Rafting in Sromowce Niżne:

Cultural Perspective: Learn about the origins and customs of rafting on the Dunajec River by visiting the Rafting Museum.

Traditional Craftsmanship: Learn about the ancient craftsmanship used in the construction of wooden rafts.

10. Customs and Culture:

Local Cuisine: Savor the customary meals and flavors of the Pieniny region's local cuisine.

Festivals and Events: Take a look at the regional celebrations of the area's cultural legacy and customs.

Beyond the thrilling Dunajec River rafting experience, Pieniny National Park has a lot more to offer. Pieniny offers a wide variety of activities and scenery to suit every visitor's interests, whether they are looking for adventure, cultural discovery, or just a peaceful getaway in the great outdoors.

5. Adventure Awaits

Trekking and Hiking

Trekking and hiking are engaging outdoor pursuits that let people push their physical limits, discover new places, and establish a connection with the natural world. Hiking pathways that suit different skill levels and tastes can be found all around the world, regardless of experience level. This is a thorough guide that goes over the fundamentals of trekking and hiking:

1. Selecting Your Path:

Difficulty Levels: Trails are divided into groups according to their degree of difficulty, which ranges from easy to challenging. Select a trail based on your level of experience and fitness.

Duration: Take into account the trail's length and the number of days you want to spend trekking. Trekking for several days and short day hikes provide distinct experiences.

2. Essential Equipment:

Footwear: Get supportive, cozy, and terrain-appropriate hiking footwear. Take them on a longer hike after breaking them in.

Clothing: Wear breathable and moisture-wicking clothes. The secret to adjusting to shifting weather conditions is layering.

Backpack: Select a well-fitting backpack that has enough room inside to hold necessities like extra layers, drinks, food, and a first aid kit.

3. Getting Around:

Compass and Maps: Acquaint yourself with trail maps and always have a compass with you. Apps for smartphones and GPS gadgets are also helpful but always have a backup plan.

Trail Markings: To stay on the correct path, pay attention to signs, cairns, and trail markings.

4. Nutrition and Hydration:

Water: Carry a sufficient amount of water with you to stay hydrated. Examine the sources of water on the walk.

Snacks: To keep your energy levels high, carry fruits, energy bars, and trail mix.

5. Safety precautions:

First Aid Kit: Keep a simple first aid kit on you at all times, filled with bandages, antiseptic wipes, and painkillers.

Emergency Contacts: Let someone know about your intended hiking route and anticipated time of return.

Weather Check: Before leaving, check the forecast and be ready for any changes in the weather.

6. Remove All Traces:

Pack it In, Pack it Out: Treat the environment with respect by disposing of all of your garbage, including tissues and food wrappers.

Stay on Designated paths: To protect the natural environment, don't build additional paths.

7. Setting Up for Fitness:

Training: Include cardiovascular, strength, and endurance activities to prepare your body for the physical demands of trekking.

Altitude Considerations: To lower the risk of altitude sickness when walking at high altitudes, acclimate gradually.

8. Hiking and trekking types:

Day hikes: are brief, frequently simple treks that can be finished in a single day.

Multi-Day Treks: Extended expeditions that need spending the night. The Appalachian Trail and the Inca Trail are two examples.

Thru-hiking: is the practice of hiking a long-distance trail from Mexico to Canada in one continuous trip.

9. Knowledge of the Environment:

Flora and Fauna: Respect the natural vegetation by keeping a safe distance and refraining from upsetting any wildlife.

Precautions for Wildlife: Be mindful of the possibility of coming into contact with wildlife and take the appropriate safety measures, including carrying bear spray.

10. Savor the Trip:

Take Breaks: Never be afraid to stop, take in the surroundings, and pay attention to your health.

Take Advantage of the Chance to Unplug from **Technology and Get Lost in Nature:** Make the most of this chance to get lost in nature.

Trekking and hiking are more than just physical pursuits; they're chances for introspection, self-realization, and appreciation of nature's splendor. A fulfilling and pleasurable experience on the trail is ensured by adhering to the fundamentals of preparation, safety, and environmental stewardship, whether you're exploring local trails or starting an international adventure.

Skiing in the Tatras

The Tatras mountain range, which separates Slovakia and Poland, provides skiers with an amazing winter experience thanks to its immaculate slopes, stunning scenery, and bustling ski resorts. The Tatras provide a wide variety of skiing options for all skill levels, from beginners to experienced skiers looking for wintertime thrills. This is a how-to guide for Tatras skiing:

1. Ski Areas:

Jasná Low Tatras, also known as Jasná Nízke Tatry:

Biggest Ski Resort: The biggest and most well-liked ski resort in Slovakia is Jasná.

Diverse Slopes: From novices to experts, there are a range of slopes available for skiing.

Modern Infrastructure: Jasná has a thriving après-ski culture, modern ski lifts, and modern facilities.

Poland's Zakopane:

Winter Capital: Situated in the High Tatra Mountains' foothills, Zakopane is referred to as Poland's winter capital.

Kasprowy Wierch: The ski area of Kasprowy Wierch offers steep slopes and breathtaking views of the Tatra Mountains.

2. Skiing Ground:

Diverse Slopes: From easy hills for novices to strenuous descents for experienced skiers, the Tatras provide a variety of slopes.

Opportunities Off-Piste: Skiers with experience can venture into backcountry skiing and off-piste terrain in specific regions.

3. Snowmobiling:

Resorts for Snowboarders: The Tatra Mountains offer terrain parks, halfpipes, and freestyle features to cater to snowboarders.

Freeriding Spots: There are some great places to go snowboarding off-piste and freeriding.

4. Ski Courses and Instruction:

Beginner-Friendly Instruction: Tatras ski schools offer instruction to newcomers, assisting them in gaining self-assurance on the slopes.

Private Instruction: For individualized guidance and skill improvement, private classes are offered.

5. Winter Occasions:

Ski contests: Throughout the winter, the Tatra Mountains hold a variety of ski contests and events that draw both professional athletes and enthusiasts.

Festivals: With music, entertainment, and cultural pursuits, winter festivals and celebrations commemorate the joy of skiing.

6. Skiing across the country:

Beautiful Paths: There are beautiful cross-country skiing paths through meadows and forests blanketed in snow in the Tatra Mountains.

High Tatras Trails: Cross-country skiers can enjoy amazing scenery on the High Tatras trails.

7. Renting Equipment:

Ski Rental Shops: Ski equipment, such as skis, boots, and poles, can be rented at ski resorts and neighboring towns.

High-quality equipment: Rental stores offer high-quality equipment appropriate for a range of skill levels and tastes.

8. Après-Ski and After Dark:

Mountain Chalets: Savor authentic local food and drinks in après-ski leisure in these classic mountain chalets and huts.

Nightlife: After a long day on the slopes, several resorts provide a lively nightlife with bars, clubs, and entertainment options.

9. Safety Points to Remember:

Safety Guidelines: Follow safety precautions, such as dressing appropriately, monitoring the weather, and just skiing at your skill level.

Avalanche Awareness: Know the safety precautions to take and heed local advice when in avalanche-prone areas.

10. Activities for a Winter Wonderland:

Snowshoeing: Use snowshoes to explore the winter wonderland and reach locations that are not accessible by designated ski slopes.

Sleigh Rides: Take a classic sleigh ride through picturesque winter scenery to truly appreciate the charm of the Tatras.

The Tatra Mountains provide the ideal combination of exhilarating slopes, breathtaking mountain scenery, and a lively winter atmosphere for skiing. The Tatra Mountains provide a wide variety of events and activities to make your winter vacation unforgettable, whether you're a skier, snowboarder, or someone looking for winter adventures.

Caving and Exploration

For individuals who are intrigued by the mysteries that lie beneath the surface of the Earth, caving and exploring underground landscapes provide a singular and interesting journey. The Tatras are a great place for caving aficionados to explore because of their complex cave systems and limestone formations. This is a guide to Tatras exploring and caving:

1. Cave Structures:

Slovakia's Demanovska Cave System:

Demanovska Ice Cave: An intriguing cave featuring stalactites, stalagmites, and unusual ice formations.

Demanovska Cave of Liberty: is well-known for its underground river and breathtaking dripstone formations.

Poland's Wielka Sniezna Cave:
The deepest cave in the Tatra Mountains is Wielka Sniezna, which draws expert cavers.

Difficult Cave Exploration: There are difficult tunnels and subterranean rooms to explore in this cave.

2. Keys to Cave Exploration:
Wear the proper safety gear, such as a helmet, gloves, a headlamp, and sturdy shoes.

Caving Suit: To guard against damp and cold temperatures, a caving suit may be required, depending on the circumstances of the cave.

First Aid Kit: Keep a little first aid kit on you in case of accidents or crises.

Three. escorted tours

Professional Guides: Participate in guided caving tours conducted by knowledgeable, seasoned guides who are acquainted with the underground systems.

Experience Learning: The guides share their knowledge of the history, geology, and special characteristics of the caverns.

4. Conservation of Caves:
Leave No Trace: To protect the delicate subterranean ecosystem, adhere to ethical

caving methods and the "leave no trace" philosophy.

Respect Wildlife: Certain species have their home in caves. Reduce the amount of disruptions to ecosystems and wildlife.

5. Cavern Types:

Ice Caves: Discover unusual ice formations in caves where frozen stalactites and stalagmites evoke a surreal mood.

Solution Caves: Often including complex structures, solution caves are created when soluble rocks, like limestone, dissolve.

6. Surveying and Mapping Caves:

Mapping Tools: Use instruments such as laser rangefinders and compasses to map and survey caves.

Contributions to Science: By taking part in cave mapping initiatives, amateur cavers can provide important data to scientific research.

7. Photographing caves:

Photographic Challenges: Overcome obstacles like dim lighting and unusual geological formations to capture the splendor of the deep world.

Respect Lighting Rules: Adhere to recommendations to reduce flash photography's negative effects on cave ecosystems.

8. Clubs and Organizations in Speleology:

Community Engagement: To meet other cavers who share your interests, sign up for regional or worldwide speleology clubs and associations.

possibilities for Training: These organizations frequently offer seminars, new cave exploration initiatives, and possibilities for training.

9. Rivers and waterfalls underground:

Subterranean Water Features: Some caverns have underground waterfalls and rivers, which give the caving experience a whole new level.

Water Passage Navigation: It is possible for cavers to have to navigate via water channels, which adds an exciting and difficult element to their exploration.

10. Physical well-being:

Endurance Training: There is a physical component to caving. Strength training and cardiovascular workouts can help you gain endurance.

Flexibility: It takes flexibility to be able to move through narrow spaces. Include stretches as part of your regimen.

Discovering a secret world of delights can be experienced through caving in the Tatra

Mountains. The Tatras provide a unique experience for caving lovers, ranging from intricate cave systems that test exploring abilities to ice caverns with shimmering patterns. Accept the spirit of exploration, be mindful of the subterranean surroundings, and relish the excitement of unlocking the secrets tucked away beneath the peaks.

Thermal Springs and Wellness

Thermal springs that promote well-being and relaxation can be found in the Tatras region, which is renowned for its varied landscapes and natural beauty. This is a guide to discovering Tatras thermal springs and wellness:

1. Poprad, Slovakia's AquaCity:

Thermal Pools: There are both indoor and outdoor thermal pool options at AquaCity Poprad.

Wellness Center: This facility has several treatment rooms, saunas, and rest areas.

2. Slovakia's Tatralandia:

Aquapark and Wellness: Tatralandia is a water park featuring wellness amenities and thermal pools.

Sauna World: Traditional and fragrant saunas are among the many sauna experiences available at Sauna World in Tatralandia.

3. Poland's Bukowina Tatrzańska:

Thermal Baths: The Poland-based Bukovina Thermal Baths feature thermal pools surrounded by picturesque mountain vistas.

Spa and Wellness: For rest and treatments, the building has a spa and wellness center.

4. Natural Springs in the High Tatras:

Štrbské Pleso: Known for its medicinal characteristics, Štrbské Pleso is a glacial mountain lake with natural thermal springs.

Unwind in the Surroundings: Soak in the warmth of the thermal springs while taking in the breathtaking scenery of the High Tatras.

5. Health and Spa Services:

Massage Therapies: Hot stone massages and aromatherapy are among the massage therapies provided by wellness centers in the Tatra Mountains.

Treatments for the Face and Body: Rejuvenate yourself with body and facial treatments.

6. Experiences in saunas:

Finnish Saunas: Experience the traditional Finnish sauna, renowned for its healing properties and dry heat.

Herbal Saunas: For a sensory experience, several wellness centers include herbal saunas with enticing aromas.

7. Yoga and Intentionality:

Yoga Classes: Experience the health benefits of yoga in peaceful settings while taking in the surrounding scenery.

Meditation Areas: A few wellness centers offer areas specifically designed for mindfulness exercises and meditation.

8. Natural Environment:

Mountain Views: Take use of wellness services and thermal springs while taking in the breathtaking scenery of the Tatra Mountains.

Outdoor Relaxation Areas: You can relax outside in the clean mountain air with a lot of amenities.

9. Resorts and Hotels:

Wellness Packages: Several lodging establishments in the Tatra Mountains provide access to thermal springs and spa services as part of their wellness packages.

Luxurious Accommodations: Revel in opulent lodgings complete with on-site spa services.

10. Seasonal Retreats for Wellbeing:

Seasonal Programs: Wellness centers might host retreats with a seasonal emphasis, including mindfulness, fitness, or detox.

Holistic Wellness: Learn about programs that combine several approaches to promote overall well-being.

Discovering wellness and thermal springs in the Tatras offers a calming fusion of the natural world with aesthetic appeal. The Tatra Mountains provide a variety of possibilities to meet your wellness needs, whether you prefer the cutting-edge amenities of aqua parks or the healing powers of natural springs. Spend some time relaxing in the serene surroundings of this charming mountainous area, allowing your body and mind to be renewed.

6. Culinary Delights

Customary Slovakian Food

The diverse cultural influences and history of Slovakia are reflected in its cuisine. Traditional Slovak cuisine frequently uses foods that are readily available in the area and are substantial and tasty. The following is a list of some of the main components of traditional Slovak food:

1. Halušky Bryndzové:

Description: Often regarded as the national cuisine, bryndzové halušky are little potato dumplings covered with crispy bacon and served with sheep cheese (bryndza).

Remarks: This is a hearty dish that highlights the usage of dairy, which is a big component in Slovak cooking.

2. Takeuchi:

Description: Typically cooked with sauerkraut, various meats (bacon, sausage), mushrooms, and paprika for taste, kapustnica is a substantial and flavorful cabbage soup.

Remarks: This meal is well-liked around Christmas and other joyous events.

3. Placky Zemiakové:

Description: Zemiakové placky are potato pancakes made with flour, eggs, and other seasonings combined with grated potatoes. Fry them till they get golden brown.

Remarks: Served with applesauce or sour cream as a light supper or as a side dish.

4. Pasquale Buchty:

Description: Steamed buns with sweet fillings like jam, crushed almonds, or poppy seeds are known as parené buchty.

Remarks: A delicious treat or sugary nibble that's appreciated on different days.

5. Lokōe

Description: Lokše are thin potato pancakes that are frequently stuffed with bryndza cheese or goose liver.

Remarks: An adaptable dish that can be had as an appetizer or a main course.

6. Takeuchi:

Description: This is a fresh cabbage soup, similar to kapustnica, that frequently has smoked pork, sausage, and mushrooms in it.

Remarks: There are varieties of kapustnica with distinct regional inf

7. Rezeň:

Description: Rezeň is the name for a breaded and deep-fried cutlet that is often made with chicken or pig.

Remarks: This is a traditional main meal, best served with side dishes like potato salad or mashed potatoes.

8. Pirate:

Description: Pirohy are dumplings stuffed with cheese, pork, potatoes, or other items. Usually, they are sautéed after being boiled.

Remarks: Serve with sour cream as a side dish or as a main course.

9. Guláš:

Description: Guláš is a robust stew consisting of beef or pig, onions, and a flavorful sauce with a strong paprika foundation.

Remarks: Frequently accompanied by bread or knedča (dumplings).

10. Tradlník:

Description: Trdelník is a popular sweet pastry, not Slovak in origin, but prepared by wrapping dough around a cylindrical spit, grilling it, and then covering it with almonds and sugar.

Remarks: Often served as a dessert or as street food.

11. Zmrzlina Demänovská:

Description: The thick and creamy texture of Demänovská zmrzlina, a typical Slovak ice cream, is well-known.

Remarks: Local foods like berries, honey, and nuts are frequently used in flavors.

The agricultural legacy of the nation and the influence of surrounding Central European countries are reflected in traditional Slovak cuisine. Slovak cuisine offers a taste of the country's cultural richness and celebrates the flavors of the region with anything from robust stews to sweet sweets.

Must-Try Dishes

It's a delightful adventure to discover Slovak food, and there are a few dishes you just must try to experience the distinctive flavors and culinary customs of the nation. The following is a list of foods you should try when visiting Slovakia:

1. Bryndzové Halušky:

Description: Potato dumplings topped with crispy bacon and served with a unique sheep cheese known as bryndza.

Why Try: Known as the national dish, it showcases the significance of dairy in Slovak cuisine with its ideal combination of flavors and textures.

2. Kapustnica:

Description: A Robust cabbage soup enhanced with paprika, sauerkraut, and different meats.

Why Try: Rich and soothing in flavor, kapustnica is a festive dish commonly associated with Christmas.

3. Zemiakové Placky:

Description: Potato pancakes cooked in a skillet till golden brown, using grated potatoes, flour, and eggs.

Why Try: Served with applesauce or sour cream, these crispy pancakes make a great side dish.

4. Lokše:

Description: Lightly fried potato pancakes stuffed with geese or bryndza cheese.

Why Try: With both savory and sweet varieties, Lokše demonstrates the diversity of potatoes in Slovak cuisine.

5. Pirohy:

Description: Dumplings stuffed with cheese, pork, potatoes, or other items and frequently eaten with sour cream.

Why Try: There are several flavor profiles available in the filling options, and pirohy is a traditional comfort meal.

6. Demänovská Zmrzlina:

Description: Traditional Slovak ice cream with a thick, creamy texture and a tendency to incorporate regional flavors.

Why Try: Savor the delicious flavor of Demänovská zmrzlina, which can be enhanced with berries, almonds, or honey.

7. Halušky s Tvarohom:

Description: Essentially little halušky-like potato dumplings, these are served with sugar and tvaroh (cottage cheese).

Why Try: A straightforward yet delectable delicacy that emphasizes the dairy ingredients used in Slovak pastries.

8. Guláš:

Description: A hearty stew with onions, thick paprika-based sauce, and beef or pig.

Why Try: Served with bread or dumplings, guláš is a tasty and fulfilling dish.

9. Demänovský Kútik:

Description: A layered cake with custard, whipped cream, and sponge cake.

Why Try: Slovak dessert skill is exhibited in the delicious delicacy Demänovský kútik.

10. Kofola:

Description: A well-liked Slovak soft drink with a distinct flavor that is frequently picked above worldwide cola brands.

Why Try: Kofola, a beloved Slovak beverage, is a great way to learn about the local drinking culture.

11. Langoš:

Description: Fried flatbread that is frequently covered with shredded cheese, ketchup, and garlic.

Why Try: A tasty and fulfilling street food snack, langoš is widely enjoyed.

12. Slovak Cheeses:

Description: Taste a range of Slovak cheeses, such as bryndza, oštiepok (smoked sheep cheese), and different varieties made from cow's milk.

Why Try: Traditional Slovak cheeses have unique flavors and textures that will appeal to cheese aficionados.

A variety of dishes in Slovakian cuisine encapsulate the essence of the nation's culinary legacy. A mouthwatering introduction to Slovakian cuisine may be had by sampling these must-try meals, which range from savory favorites like bryndzové halušky to sweet delicacies like lokše.

Local Markets and Food Experiences

A fascinating excursion into Slovakia's culinary heritage can be had by visiting local markets, which offer a view of the lively assortment of fresh produce, artisanal products, and regional delicacies. Here are a few local culinary markets and experiences in Slovakia that you should not miss:

Location: Bratislava

Highlights

Fresh Produce: Browse tables piled high with locally produced dairy goods, fruits, and vegetables.

Artisanal Goods: Sample regional cheeses, handcrafted items, and classic Slovak cuisine.

2. The Central Market (Stredisko Bratislava): Location: Bratislava

Highlights:

Meat and Sausages: Try and buy a range of sausages, cured meats, and fresh meats.

Bakery Delights: Indulge in the smells of freshly made pastries and bread from neighborhood bakeries.

3. Old Market Hall (Stará Tržnica):
 Location: Bratislava

Highlights:

Farmers' Market: Take advantage of the regularly scheduled Farmers' Market, which offers locally sourced goods and organic produce.

Gourmet Food: Take a look at the various gourmet food stands that serve anything from Slovak to international cuisines.

4. Košice Market Hall (Košický Trhový Dom): Location: Košice

Highlights:

Regional Specialties: Take a look at the cheeses, sausages, and other regional specialties of Eastern Slovakia.

Fresh Fish Market: Košice Market Hall is well-known for its seafood-showcasing fresh fish market.

5. Market Square in Banská Bystrica:

Location: Banská Bystrica

Highlights:

Local Crafts: Peruse booths showcasing handcrafted goods, souvenirs, and traditional Slovak crafts.

Street Food: Savor regional snacks and sweets among the street food options.

6. Liptovský Mikuláš Market:

Location: Liptovský Mikuláš Market

Highlights:

Regional Flavors: Taste the regional specialties from the Liptov region by visiting the stalls offering dairy and meat goods.

Culinary Events: Take part in the market's food festivals and culinary events.

7. Farmers' Market in Oravská Lesná:

Location: Oravská Lesná

Highlights:

Local Honey: Sample and buy premium honey from local beekeepers in the area.

Fresh Vegetables: Get a range of seasonal, fresh vegetables directly from nearby growers.

8. Pieŷťany Market Square:

Location: Piešťany

Highlights:

Local Wine and Spirits: Visit vendors selling liqueurs, wines, and spirits from the area.

Confectionery: Savor delectable pastries and candies from nearby bakeries.

9. Trenčín Farmers' Market:

Location: Trenčín

Highlights:

Artisanal Cheeses: Local dairy farmers offer a variety of artisanal cheeses that you can sample.

Buy Handmade mementos: Treat yourself to presents and mementos that honor Trenčín's rich cultural past.

10. Customary Celebrations and Culinary Activities:

Location: Various regions

Highlights:

Food Festivals: Take part in customary food festivals that highlight local cuisine and culinary customs.

Cultural Celebrations: Attend regional cuisine, music, and cultural festivals.

Learning about regional cuisine and marketplaces in Slovakia offers a clear window into the nation's gastronomic character. Every market, whether it be in a charming hamlet square or a busy metropolitan market, offers a different range of goods, tastes, and cultural experiences that add to the complex tapestry of Slovak cuisine.

Wine and Spirits

Slovakia's viticultural heritage and the skill of its regional distillers are the foundation of the country's growing wine and spirits industry. A guide to the wide world of Slovak wine and spirits is provided here:

Drink:

Slovakia has a long history of producing a wide variety of wines from its several wine regions. Examine the distinctive qualities of Slovak wines:

1. Wine Region of Tokaj:

Famous for: Noble rot (botrytis cinerea), a unique manufacturing method used to create the sweet wine Tokaj.

Notable Varietals: Yellow Muscat, Lipovina, and Furmint.

2. Tiny Wine Region in the Carpathians:

Famous for: Manufacturing a large amount of Slovakian wine, which is renowned for its crisp whites and robust reds.

Notable Varietals: Frankovka (Blaufränkisch), Welschriesling, and Grüner Veltliner.

3. Wine Region of Nitra:

Famous for: Nitra, a location with a lot of promise, is concentrated on producing high-quality white wines.

Notable Varietals: Grüner Veltliner and Müller-Thurgau

4. Sparkling wines from Slovakia:

Description: Slovakia is known for producing high-quality sparkling wines, some of which are made using age-old techniques.

Notable Varietals: Pinot Noir and Chardonnay

Spirits:

Slovakia is renowned for its traditional spirits, which are frequently expertly made and encapsulate Slovak culture:

1. Bogdanovička:

Description: Borovička is a traditional Slovak drink with floral and piney aromas, made from juniper brandy or gin.

Serving: Naked or as a mixer for mixed drinks.

2. Slovićka:

Description: Slivovica is a well-known traditional spirit made from plums that has a rich fruity flavor and a high alcohol level.

Serving: Try it neat or add it to a variety of recipes.

3. The Hruskovica

Description: Hruskovica, or pear brandy, is a popular digestive that embodies the flavor of ripe pears.

Serving: After a meal, sip modest amounts.

4. Mazemák:

Description: Sugar beets and molasses are used to make Tuzemák, a traditional Slovak rum.

Serving: Add it to drinks or eat it by itself.

5. The Demänovka

Description: Demänovka is an herbal liqueur that has a distinct and nuanced flavor because of the combination of herbs and spices.

Serving: Usually taken as an afterthought.

Wine and Spirits Tastings:

Discover the wine and spirits of Slovakia through interactive experiences:

1. Tours for Wine Tasting:

Guided Tours: Join guided wine-tasting tours in the major wine districts to learn about the area's cellars and vineyards.

Varietal Exploration: Taste a range of Slovak wines, from bold reds to fragrant whites, as part of your varietal exploration.

2. Visits to Local Distilleries:

Craft Distilleries: Visit regional distilleries that produce classic spirits like Slivovica and Borovička.

Distillery Tour: Take a distillery tour to discover the craft of making Slovak spirits and the distillation process.

3. Events that Pair Wine with Food:

Wine Dinners: To enjoy the harmony of flavors, go to wine and food-matching events at vineyards or restaurants.

Local Cuisine: Discover how traditional Slovak cuisine goes well with Slovak wines.

4. Festivals of Wine and Spirits:

Local Events: Take part in cultural celebrations and new release discoveries by visiting wine and spirits festivals hosted around Slovakia.

Meet Producers: Learn about the skills of winemakers and distillers by getting to know them.

The wine and spirits industry in Slovakia presents a diverse range of tastes, customs, and encounters. Every experience offers a glimpse of the varied and vibrant beverage culture of the nation, whether you're savoring a glass of Tokaj while gazing over vine-covered hills or taking in the warmth of Slivovica at a neighborhood pub.

7. Unique Experiences

Medieval Castle Tours

There are many medieval castles in Slovakia, each with a distinct history and attractive architecture. By exploring these castles, guests can take a step back in time and become fully immersed in the area's medieval past. This is a list of some of Slovakia's most important medieval castles to see:

1. Castle Spiš:

Location: Close to Podhradie Spišské

Highlights:

UNESCO World Heritage Site: Spiš Castle is a UNESCO World Heritage Site and one of Europe's largest castle complexes.

Panoramic vistas: From the castle's elevated perch, take in breathtaking vistas of the surrounding landscape.

Historical Exhibitions: Take in the inside of the castle through displays of medieval relics.

2. Crown of Bojnice:

Location: Bojnice

Highlights:

Romantic Architecture: The romantic, fairytale-like architecture of Bojnice Castle is well known.

Bojnice Castle Museum: Explore the historical collections and displays housed within the castle.

Experience the International Ghosts and Spirits Festival, which takes place annually at Bojnice Castle.

3. Castle Orava:

Location: Oravský Podzámok.

Highlights:

Dramatic Setting: Orava Castle has an imposing and dramatic presence as it perches atop a tall rock.

Folk Architecture Museum: Discover the Folk Architecture Museum at the castle, which features exhibits on traditional rural Slovak life.

Movie Location: Orava Castle became well-known as a filming site for the iconic film "Nosferatu."

4. Castle Trenčín:

Location: Trenčín

Highlights:

Strategic Position: Trenčín Castle is positioned advantageously atop a steep rock that provides a panoramic view of the town below.

Roman Inscription: Explore the Roman inscription "Laugaricio," which is among the oldest in Slovakia.

Interactive Exhibits: Visitors can participate in interactive activities and displays at the castle.

5. The Devin Castle

Location: Bratislava

Highlights:

Danube River Views: Devin Castle is located at the meeting point of the Danube and Morava rivers and provides breathtaking views.

Archeological Site: Discover millennia of history by exploring the archeological site located within the castle grounds.

Folk Performances: Enjoy the folk activities and performances that are customarily hosted at the castle in Slovakia.

6. Castle Čachtice:

Location: Čachtice

Highlights:

Elizabeth Báthory: The notorious Countess Elizabeth Báthory is linked to Čachtice Castle.

Ruined Atmosphere: The remains of the castle produce an eerie atmosphere.

Hiking routes: Beautiful hiking routes lead to the castle.

7. Budapest Castle:

Location: Bratislava

Highlights:

City Views: The Bratislava Castle provides sweeping views of the Danube River and the city.

History Museum: See the historical displays of Slovak culture and history in the castle's history museum.

Baroque Gardens: Wander through the stunning Baroque Gardens that encircle the castle.

8. Castle of Strečno:

Location: Strreno

Highlights:

Picturesque Setting: The picturesque setting of Strečno Castle is complemented by the Váh River and beautiful scenery.

Medieval Exhibitions: View the medieval exhibits at the castle, which feature relics and weapons from the era.

Outdoor Events: The castle holds festivals and outdoor reenactments of medieval life.

Tips for Castles Tours:

Guided Tours: If you want to learn more about the background and legends of each castle, think about taking one of the guided tours.

Seasonal Events: To enhance your experience at the castle, look for seasonal events like medieval festivals or cultural shows.

Hiking routes: If you're looking for an exciting way to explore, certain castles may be reached via beautiful hiking routes.

Discovering Slovakia's medieval castles is a chance to take in the breathtaking scenery, architectural wonders, and rich cultural legacy that characterize the nation's castle landscape.

Traditional Handicrafts

Slovakia has a thriving handcraft culture, with talented craftspeople creating a vast array of traditional goods that honor the nation's cultural past. These hand-crafted gems frequently have a strong relationship with Slovak history, tradition, and craftsmanship. The following is a list of some of the customary handicrafts that may be found in Slovakia:

1. Carving in Wood:

Description: The centuries-old art of Slovak wood carving is renowned for its elaborate designs. Beautifully carved wooden sculptures, furniture, and decorative objects are made by artisans.

Popular Items: Wooden spoons, figures, religious carvings, and elaborately carved furniture.

2. Ceramics:

Description: Vibrant colors and distinctive patterns characterize traditional Slovak ceramics. Artists frequently employ methods like sgraffito and slip trailing to produce unique designs.

Popular Items: Folk-themed ornamental tiles, bowls, mugs, and plates.

3. Lace Making:

Description: Making lace, particularly bobbin lace, is a painstaking art that has been handed down through the years. Detailed floral and geometric designs are frequently depicted in lacework.

Popular Items: Lace accessories, tablecloths, and doilies.

4. Needlework:

Description: An important aspect of Slovak textile traditions is embroidery. There are regional variations in needlework designs that use vivid hues and meaningful symbols.

Popular Items: Decorative textiles, blouses, and folk costumes (kroje).

5. Pasanky Easter Eggs:

Description: A Slovak Easter custom is the skill of piasanky or egg decoration. Eggs are patterned with wax and dye intricacies.

Popular Items: Easter egg displays decorated for the holiday.

6. Pottery:

Description: In Slovakia, creating pottery is a common craft. Earthy colors and practical patterns are hallmarks of traditional pottery.

Popular Items: Ceramic cookware, pitchers, and clay pots.

7. Weaving Baskets:

Description: Weaving baskets is a traditional technique that involves using natural materials, such as straw or willow, to create decorative and utilitarian objects.

Popular Items: Weaved bags, baskets, and ornamental objects.

8. Leatherworking:

Description: To make elaborate designs, Slovak leathercraft frequently uses hand tooling and embossing leather. It's usual to employ traditional symbols and patterns.

Popular Items: Purses, wallets, belts, and adorned leather accessories.

9. Blowing Glass:

Description: Slovakia has a long tradition of producing glass. Expert craftspeople use brilliant colors and classic patterns to make hand-blown glass products.

Popular Items: Glassware, decorations, and ornamental

10. Jewels with Filigree:

Description: Detailed wirework is required to make delicate and elaborate components while creating filigree jewelry. Folk themes are a common feature of traditional Slovak designs.

Popular Items: Brooches, necklaces, and earrings.

11. Cookies with honey (Medovníky):

Description: Medovníky are spiced and honey-baked cookies that resemble gingerbread. They are frequently beautifully adorned with vibrant frosting.

Popular Items: Honey sweets with decorations that are served for festivities and special events.

Tips for Purchasing Traditional Handicrafts:

Visit Craft Markets: Take a look at the handcrafted goods that local craftsmen are selling at craft fairs and markets.

Promote Artisan Shops: Look for studios and artisan stores that focus on creating traditional handicrafts.

Ask About Techniques: Talk to artists to discover the methods and inspirations behind their creations.

Bringing traditional Slovak handicrafts home helps to preserve these ancient customs in addition to letting you possess a one-of-a-kind work of art. Every handicraft, whether it's a piece of exquisitely embroidered fabric or a gorgeously carved wooden figurine, reveals something new about Slovakia's rich cultural heritage.

Village Stays

A village stay in Slovakia offers a singular chance to become fully immersed in the rich cultural legacy of the nation and establish a personal connection with the welcoming rural inhabitants. This is a guide to Slovakian village stays:

Choose a Charming Village:

Selection: Whether it's nestled in the mountains, next to a historic monument, or surrounded by nature, do your homework and pick a charming community that suits your interests.

2. Accommodations:

Guesthouses and Homestays: Choose one of these accommodations for a genuine experience. Many times, local families that manage these lodgings offer a kind and individualized touch.

Rural Cottages: You may experience the simplicity of village life by staying in one of the rustic cottages available in several settlements.

3. Local Cuisine:

Home-cooked dishes: Savor authentic Slovak dishes made by your hosts with ingredients that are acquired locally.

Cooking lessons: Learn the craft of making Slovak cuisine by enrolling in one of the cooking lessons offered by some village hotels.

4. Cultural Activities:

Folk Performances: Take in traditional dance and music from Slovakia, presented by your local communities.

Craft Workshops: Learn traditional handicrafts from local artisans by taking part in craft workshops.

5. Investigate Nature:

Guided Nature hikes: Discover the natural splendor and learn about the native flora and wildlife by going on guided hikes in the surrounding area.

Outdoor Activities: Take part in outdoor pursuits offered by the community, such as hiking, cycling, or horseback riding.

6. Events and Festivals:

Local Celebrations: See whether any festivals or other events are scheduled in your area during your visit, providing an opportunity to join in the celebration with the locals.

Seasonal Celebrations: Take part in customary celebrations that are tied to the seasons, the harvest, or regional traditions.

7. Cultural Locations:

Village Heritage: Take a tour of the village's historical sites, which include landmarks, old churches, and traditional homes.

Guided Tours: Schedule a guided tour to discover the cultural significance and historical background of the village.

8. Grand Tours:

Rural Farm Experience: Take a tour of nearby farms to see how they operate daily, discover more about farming methods and even take part in farm activities.

Cheesemaking or Brewing: Certain villages have a focus on age-old crafts such as brewing or cheesemaking. Investigate these procedures directly.

9. Involvement in Community:

Talk with Locals: Have discussions with the villages to discover more about their customs, way of life, and folklore.

Take Part in Local activities: Attend communal activities or get-togethers to temporarily integrate with the community.

10. Slowing Down and Thinking:

Calm Retreat: Take time to relax in serene surroundings, far from the bustle of cities, and embrace the peace of village life.

Scenic Views: Take in breathtaking views of the surrounding area while lounging on a terrace or in a village garden.

Advice for Stays in Villages:

Reserve in Advance: Village stays fill up quickly, so it's best to reserve your lodging in advance.

Respect Local Customs: To ensure a peaceful encounter, be mindful of local customs and traditions.

Learn Basic Phrases: Acquire a basic vocabulary of Slovak phrases to help you communicate and demonstrate your respect for the language.

In Slovakia, staying in a village provides an opportunity to get off the typical tourist routes and experience the essence of the nation. It's an adventure into the heart of Slovak culture, where the natural beauty and friendly people make for a very memorable experience.

Local Festivals and Events

Slovakia celebrates its rich cultural heritage, customs, and artistic creations all year long with a wide range of festivals and events. Participating in these energetic events offers a singular chance to fully engage with the local ambiance and discover the vitality of Slovak culture. This is a list of some of Slovakia's most important celebrations and events:

1. Bratislava Music Festival:
Location: Bratislava

Highlights
Classical Music: Renowned local and international orchestras and performers will be included in this esteemed classical music event.
Historic Venues: Events are held in historically significant locations, which enriches the cultural experience in general.
2. The Folklore Festival of Východná:
Location: Východná
Highlights:
Folklore Performances: Features traditional dance, music, and performances to honor Slovak folklore.
Crafts and Workshops: Offers workshops, traditional Slovak craft demonstrations, and craft displays.
3. Pohoda Celebration:
Location: Trenčín
Highlights:
Eclectic Music Lineup: One of Slovakia's biggest music events, with a wide lineup of both local and foreign performers.
Cultural Events: In addition to music, Pohoda features talks on various cultural subjects, theatrical productions, and art installations.
4. Spring Košice Music:
Location: Košice
Highlights:

Classical Music: Features concerts of classical music that draw artists from around the world as well as local performers.

Historical Venues: Košice's historic venues frequently host performances.

5. . Slovak International Air Fest (SIAF):

Location: Sliač

Highlights:

Aerial Displays: An exciting air show with both military and private aircraft, along with acrobatic performances and displays.

Aviation Enthusiasts: Attracts global aviation enthusiasts.

6. Holiday Markets:

Location: Numerous towns and cities

Highlights:

Festive Atmosphere: Take in the charming ambiance of holiday stalls, lights, and festive decorations at Christmas markets.

Handicrafts and snacks: Stop by booths selling mulled wine, regional snacks, and traditional Slovak handicrafts.

7. Festival Cerveny Kamen:

Location: Červený Kame\ Castle

Highlights:

Historical Reenactments: This feature brings the history of the castle to life through historical reenactments.

Crafts and Workshops: This section features workshops, craft demonstrations, and activities with a medieval theme.

8. Wine Festivals in Slovakia:

Location: Numerous wine regions

Highlights:

Wine Tasting: Enjoy Slovak wine production during wine-tasting events, which frequently feature nearby vineyards.

Cultural Events: Take part in wine celebrations with local cuisine, music, and traditional dances.

9. International Spirits and Ghosts Festival:

Location: Castle Bojnice

Highlights:

Magical ambiance: This festival, which takes place at Bojnice Castle, evokes a mystical ambiance with its ghostly acts, parades, and fairy tale-themed activities.

Costumed Participants: To enhance the enchanted atmosphere, visitors are welcome to dress in costume.

10. Festivals at Dobšinská Ice Cave:

Location: Dobšinská Ice Cave**

Highlights:

Ice Sculptures: Highlights the wonders of the cave's organic ice formations, frequently with ice sculpture exhibits.

Guided Tours: Throughout the festival, unique guided tours and events are planned.

Advice for Attending Festivals:

Verify Dates: Since festival dates can change annually, make sure you check them in advance.

Buy Tickets Early: If an event requires a ticket, think about buying them in advance, particularly for well-known festivals.

Plan Accommodations: Make reservations as soon as possible, particularly if the festival draws a sizable crowd.

Taking part in celebrations that highlight Slovakia's rich traditions and artistic expressions, engaging with the local culture, and enjoying a variety of performances are all made possible by attending festivals and events around the country.

8. Practical Travel Tips

Transportation Guide

Reliable and efficient transportation is essential for experiencing Slovakia's attractive cities and navigating its varied terrain. Here is a transportation guide to make your travels across the nation easier:

1. Public Transportation:

Buses: Slovakia boasts a vast bus network that links towns, cities, and even outlying places. A practical and affordable way to see the nation is by bus.

Trains: Slovakia's well-developed railway network offers effective links between its major cities. It's a cozy choice for extended travels.

2. Rent a Car:

Renting a Car: If you choose to rent a car, you'll have more freedom to see Slovakia at your speed, particularly in rural areas and places with little access to public transportation.

Roads: While most rural Slovakian roads are kept up, some may be more narrow and twisty. Verify the state of the roads, particularly in the winter.

3. Taxis:

Urban Taxis: Cities like Bratislava and Košice have an abundance of taxis. To guarantee reasonable prices, use trustworthy cab services or applications.

Rural Areas: It's best to book cabs in advance in remote locations.

4. Cycling

Bike Rentals: You may explore metropolitan areas and picturesque landscapes on two wheels by renting a bike from several cities and tourist destinations.

Riding paths: There is a network of riding paths across Slovakia, particularly in national parks and by rivers.

5. Domestic Flights:

Air Travel: Slovakia has few internal flights despite its small size. When traveling domestically, most people choose ground transportation.

6. Boats and Ferries:

Danube River: The Danube River is home to ferries and boats that provide beautiful rides and connect the cities that line its banks.

7.Tours Guided:

Tour Packages: Take into account guided tours for particular areas or sites. Transportation is frequently included with these tours, which makes it convenient for guests.

8. Passes for Travel:

Public Transportation Passes: To save money, look into regional or national travel passes if you intend to use public transportation frequently.

Transportation Advice:

Language: Even though English is widely used in cities, it can be useful to know some fundamental Slovak words, particularly in rural areas.

Currency: Keep local money (Euro) on hand to pay for transportation, particularly in farther-flung areas.

Travel applications: For up-to-date schedules, routes, and reservation information, use transportation applications.

Specifics for Cities:

1. Bratislava

Public Transport: Buses and trams are part of Bratislava's effective public transportation network. Purchase tickets using mobile apps or in advance.

Walking: Walking is an excellent way to explore the city center because it is compact and pedestrian-friendly.

2. Košice:

Public Transport: Buses and trams are available for usage in Košice. At stops, there are vending machines for tickets.

Bike-Friendly: With dedicated bike lanes in select locations, Košice is a bike-friendly city.

3. Poprad—the entry point to the High Tatras:

Train Connections: Poprad is an ideal starting point for touring the High Tatras because it is a significant railway hub. Trains go to several locations.

Bystrica Banska:

Compact City: The city center of Banska Bystrica is small, making foot exploration enjoyable. There are local buses that go to the nearby communities.

5. Nitra

Public Transportation: The public bus system in Nitra operates. There are also ride-sharing and taxi options available.

Slovakia provides a range of transit choices to accommodate various tastes and modes of travel. You can discover an appropriate means of transportation to visit this enchanting nation, whether you favor the freedom of a rental car, the ease of public transportation, or the gorgeous paths of cycling.

Accommodation Options

Slovakia provides a wide variety of lodging choices to suit all tastes and price ranges. This is a list of the many kinds of lodging in Slovakia:

1. Hotels:

Luxury Hotels: There are luxury hotels with upscale amenities, spas, and fine dining alternatives in major cities like Bratislava and Košice.

Business Hotels: Designed with business travelers in mind, these lodging options frequently offer easy access to highways, meeting spaces, and fast internet.

2. B&Bs and guesthouses:

Charming Guesthouses: Cozy guest houses providing a more private and individualized experience can be found in smaller towns and rural locations.

Bed and Breakfasts (B&Bs): These lodging options frequently include a home-cooked breakfast as well as a cozy, welcoming environment.

3. Lodgings:

Cost-Effective: Hostels are an affordable choice, particularly for individuals traveling alone or on a limited budget.

Shared Accommodations: Hostels usually provide shared facilities in the form of dormitory-style rooms.

4. Vacation Rentals and Apartments:

Self-Catering Apartments: With extra space and a kitchen for increased convenience, apartments are perfect for people who want to cook for themselves.

Vacation Homes: Charming vacation homes that offer a peaceful haven can be found in rural places.

5. Resorts

Mountain Resorts: You may find mountain resorts that combine pleasant lodging, spa treatments, and outdoor activities in areas like the High Tatras.

Wellness Resorts: A few resorts include spa services and treatments with an emphasis on relaxation and well-being.

6. Penzións:

Traditional Lodging: Penzións are tiny, family-run lodging options that can be found all around Slovakia and provide a genuine, local experience.

Local Cuisine: Traditional Slovak dinners may be offered by certain penzións.

7. upscale hotels:

Unique Design: Slovakian boutique hotels frequently have distinctive ambiances, individualized service, and unique designs.

Central Locations: Since they are usually located in the middle of things, it is simple to visit neighboring attractions.

8. Farm Stays & Agritourism:

Rural Experience: Spend time on a farm to get a taste of rural Slovak life. This kind of lodging offers a first-hand look at agricultural operations.

Local Produce: Visitors may be able to partake in farm-related activities and savor fresh produce.

9. Campsites:

Nature Camping: Due to its stunning natural surroundings, Slovakia is a great place for campers. There are campsites in many beautiful places.

Caravan Parks: A few campgrounds also welcome campers with caravans.

10. University Housing:

Cheap-Friendly: Dormitories may be accessible throughout the summer in university towns, offering an affordable lodging choice.

Basic Amenities: For a budget-friendly stay, dorms typically provide the necessities.

A Guide to Selecting Lodging:

Location: Take into account the area's general atmosphere, accessibility to public transit, and nearby attractions.

Budget: Establish your spending limit and look at possibilities that fall into that area.

Reviews: Examine other passengers' comments to determine the caliber of the lodging.

Amenities: List the amenities that are most important to you, such as breakfast, free parking, or Wi-Fi.

Reservation Sites:

Booking.com

Airbnb

Hostels.com

Asylum World

Slovakia has many lodging options to improve your trip, whether you're looking for elegance, the warmth of kind locals, or affordable solutions. You can select a place that fits your preferences, from guesthouses in rural areas surrounded by nature to historic hotels in city centers.

Currency and Banking

Slovakia's official currency as of January 2022, according to my most recent information update, is the Euro (EUR). It's crucial to remember that information about currencies is subject to change, therefore for the most recent information, I advise contacting nearby banks or consulting a trustworthy source.

Here are some basic details about money and banks in Slovakia:

Currency:
Coin Code: Euro (EUR)
Symbol: Euro
Subunits: There are 100 cents in each euro.
Coins and Banknotes:
Notebooks: Typical notes come in the following denominations: €5, €10, €20, €50, €100, €200, and €500.
Coins: Coins are available in €1 and €2 denominations in addition to 1, 2, 5, 10, 20, and 50 cent values.
ATMs:
Availability: Towns, cities, and tourist destinations all have a good supply of ATMs (Automated Teller Machines).
Accepted Cards: ATMs typically accept major debit and credit cards.
Bank Card:
Acceptance: In cities, hotels, restaurants, and bigger institutions, credit cards (such as Visa, MasterCard, and, to a lesser extent, American Express) are frequently accepted.
Notify Your Bank: To prevent possible problems with card transactions, let your bank know about your travel dates and destination before you depart.
Banking Locations and Hours:
Banking Hours: Generally, banks in Slovakia are open from 8:00 AM to 4:00 PM, Monday

through Friday. On Fridays, some branches might close early.

Currency Exchange: You can exchange currencies at exchange offices and banks. Larger cities and airports typically feature several exchange sites.

Tips for Currency Exchange:

Exchange Rates: Bank and official exchange office exchange rates are typically trustworthy. Steer clear of paying someone for cash on the street.

Fees: Recognize any commissions or fees related to currency exchange. Look around for the greatest price.

Passports for Travelers:

Use: Traveler's checks are not as widely accepted as they once were, so you may have trouble finding places that take them. It is advised to pay with alternative methods.

Banking via Mobile:

Apps: A lot of banks provide mobile banking apps that give users easy access to account data and a few other banking services.

Contactless Payments: Using smartwatches or cell phones, contactless payments are getting more and more popular.

A Guide to Managing Funds:

Local Currency: For minor transactions and locations that might not take credit cards, it's a good idea to have some local currency.

Notify Your Bank: To avoid any interruptions to card transactions, notify your bank of your travel arrangements.

Emergency Numbers: If you experience problems with your cards, make a note of your bank's emergency contact numbers.

Since my last update in January 2022, there may have been changes to the currency-related elements. Therefore, please confirm this information with current sources. Furthermore, certain banking policies and services could differ, so it's a good idea to speak with your bank directly to receive tailored guidance regarding your travel arrangements.

Language and Communication

Slovak is the official language of Slovakia. The following are some salient features of Slovakian language and communication:

1. Speaking Slovak:

Official Language: The language of Slovakia is Slovak.

Alphabet: The Latin alphabet is used in Slovak, with a few extra diacritical markings applied to some letters.

Grammar: Slovak is a Slavic language with distinctive linguistic characteristics. Its grammar contains elements like noun declensions and verb conjugations.

2. English Proficiency:

Urban regions: You'll discover that many individuals speak English in major cities, especially in tourist regions. This is especially true for the younger generation and those employed in the service sector.

Rural locations: Knowledge of some basic Slovak phrases can be useful as English proficiency may be less frequent in more remote or rural locations.

3. Simple Slovak Expressions:

Even when you interact with English speakers, knowing a few simple Slovak words will improve your experience and communication. Here are a few typical expressions:

Greetings: Ahoj

Farewell: Dovidenia

Gratitude: ďakujem

Yes: Áno

No: Nie

Excuse me / I'm sorry: Prepáčte

Please: Prosím

Do you speak English?: Hovoríte po anglicky?

Where is...?: Kde je...?

4. Communication Protocols:

Politeness: Slovaks value manners and, depending on the circumstance, may utilize formal titles and salutations.

Greetings: A typical way to greet someone is with a handshake. People may use titles and last names in formal settings.

Eye Contact: Keeping your eyes open is usually interpreted as a show of respect.

5. Information Centers:

Tourist Information: There are information centers in tourist locations where staff members can help with maps, brochures, and travel advice and may also speak English.

6. Language-Mixing Signs:

Public Spaces: Signage and information in public areas may be bilingual, including in English, in large cities and popular tourist locations.

7. Language Apps:

Translation Apps: If you find yourself in circumstances where English is not frequently spoken, think about utilizing translation apps.

8. Culturally Attuned:

Respect Local Customs: Although English is widely spoken in tourist locations, you can have a more authentic cultural experience by being aware of and mindful of local language and customs.

9. In Hungarian and German:

Minority Languages: Due to the existence of ethnic minorities in Slovakia, German and Hungarian are acknowledged as minority languages in some areas.

10. In sign language:

Slovak Sign Language: The deaf community uses Slovak Sign Language. Some people in metropolitan areas could know some basic sign language.

Connectivity and the Internet:

Wi-Fi: It's simple to stay connected thanks to the widespread availability of Wi-Fi in public areas, restaurants, and lodging facilities.

Mobile Data: If you anticipate using data on your phone a lot, think about purchasing a local SIM card.

Comprehending and employing fundamental Slovak expressions, particularly in more conventional or countryside locales, can enhance an all-encompassing and pleasurable encounter in Slovakia. But you'll discover that English is commonly understood in most tourist-friendly areas.

9. Responsible Travel

Eco-Friendly Initiatives

Slovakia, like many other nations, has been putting more of an emphasis on eco-friendly programs to support sustainable practices and environmental protection as of my last knowledge update in January 2022. The following are some typical environmentally friendly programs in Slovakia:

1. Renewable Energy:

Slovakia has been making investments in hydropower, solar, wind, and other renewable energy sources to lessen its reliance on non-renewable resources.

2. Protected areas and national parks:

Slovakia has several national parks and protected areas that support sustainable tourism practices and the preservation of wildlife.

3. Management of Waste:

To reduce the influence on the environment, waste reduction, recycling, and appropriate disposal of trash are being implemented.

4. Practices for Sustainable Tourism:

- The tourism sector is progressively implementing sustainable practices, like eco-friendly lodging, conscientious tour operators, and initiatives to reduce tourists' environmental impact.

5. Transportation by Public:
Enhancing and promoting public transit helps lower the number of people driving their cars and, as a result, lowers carbon emissions.

6. Green Structures:
Green building techniques and sustainable architecture are becoming more and more popular, with an emphasis on eco-friendly building materials and energy efficiency.

7. Education on the Environment:
Campaigns to educate both residents and tourists about environmental challenges and the value of conservation.

8. Preservation of Protected Species:
Conservation initiatives to save threatened species and maintain biodiversity across a range of environments.

9. Earth-friendly Activities:
The planning of environmentally friendly gatherings and festivals that emphasize resource conservation, waste minimization, and sustainability.

10. Bicycle-Friendly Projects:
To encourage environmentally friendly transportation, cities and towns are putting in place bike-friendly infrastructure, such as bike lanes and bike-sharing schemes.

11. Ecological Farming:

Initiatives to support ecologically friendly and organic farming practices, as well as other sustainable agricultural practices.

12. Eco-Accreditations:

Companies, lodging establishments, and tour guides can apply for eco-certifications to show their dedication to environmental sustainability.

13. Preservation of Forests:

Actions to stop illicit logging and promote sustainable forest management, such as replanting initiatives.

14. Conserving Water:

Programs to support appropriate water use and preserve water resources.

15. Eco-Friendly Items:

The availability and marketing of environmentally friendly products, like locally sourced goods and packaging made of biodegradable materials.

Slovakia may change over time in terms of its dedication to environmentally friendly methods, so it's important to stay up to date on the most recent developments and specific projects there. These projects are frequently led and carried out in large part by local businesses, governmental entities, and environmental organizations. If you want to visit or participate in environmentally conscious endeavors, think about learning about and endorsing companies and organizations that place a high value on sustainability.

Cultural Respect and Etiquette

When visiting Slovakia, it's important to observe national customs and manners to have a good time interacting with the people there and to take advantage of all the rich cultural experiences the nation has to offer. The following are some standards for cultural politeness and respect:

1. Greetings

Handshakes: In both formal and casual contexts, a firm handshake is customary as a greeting.

Titles and Last Names: Until a more casual relationship is established, it is courteous to use titles and last names in formal settings.

2. Courtesy and politeness:

Courtesy Is Important: Courtesy and politeness are valued by Slovaks. In daily conversations, saying "please" (prosím) and "thank you" (ďakujem) is beneficial.

Quiet Conversations: To preserve a feeling of seclusion, conversations in public spaces, such as on public transportation, are typically held at a lower volume.

3. Present-Giving Protocols:

Gifts are Appreciated: When welcomed to someone's home, it is usual to bring a modest gift. Often chosen gifts are chocolates, flowers, or a bottle of wine.

Open Gifts Later: It's courteous to open gifts you get later rather than right away in front of the giver.

4. Clothes Code:

Casual and Smart Casual: Slovaks typically wear either a casual or smart casual outfit. When dressing for a formal setting, use appropriate clothing. Avoid wearing too casual clothing.

Covering Shoulders and Knees: It is customary to cover one's shoulders and knees when entering places of worship.

5. Honoring Traditions:

Honor Folk Traditions: Slovakia boasts an abundance of folklore and customs. Even if you don't entirely comprehend a custom or event, show respect for it nonetheless.

6. Language Etiquette:

Learn Basic Phrases: Even if many Slovaks know English, it can still be beneficial to learn some basic Slovak phrases. It's common for locals to value the effort put forth in speaking their language.

Speak Moderately: To aid non-native English speakers in understanding, speak at a reasonable tempo when speaking the language.

7. Punctuality:

Be On Time: Being on time is valued, particularly in professional and corporate contexts. Be punctual for social gatherings and meetings.

8. Public Conduct:

Public Spaces: Retain a certain degree of civility in public areas. Talking too loudly or acting disruptively could be viewed as rude.

Queuing: In public areas, observe lines and wait your time.

9. Observance of Nature:

Nature Conservation: Slovakia boasts stunning scenery. Respect the environment by staying off of designated trails, disposing of waste properly, and preventing environmental harm.

10. Faith and Traditions:

Respect Religious Customs: Be mindful of regional traditions when visiting places of worship, such as taking off headgear and covering shoulders.

Easter Traditions: On Easter, take into consideration partaking in or honoring regional customs, such as the water-dousing on Easter Monday.

11. Tipping Customs:

Tipping is Common: Tipping is expected for services rendered in cafes and restaurants. It's customary to add a 10% gratuity or round up the bill.

12. Photographer Protocols:

Ask Permission: It is courteous to ask permission before taking pictures of individuals, particularly in rural locations.

13. Village Interactions:

Respect Privacy: Be considerate of others' privacy in villages. Refrain from going onto private property without authorization.

14. Taking In Invites:

Express Gratitude: Show appreciation for the invitation if you are invited to someone's house. It is a kind gesture to bring a tiny gift.

15. Smoking Protocols:

Designated Areas: Enclosed public areas are off-limits to smoking. Be considerate of others and only smoke in approved areas.

It's not only more enjoyable to travel when you follow cultural customs and etiquette, but it also helps you build good relationships with locals. Respecting Slovak norms and traditions goes a long way in building real connections, even if many Slovaks are tolerant of cultural differences and open-minded.

Supporting Local Communities

One great approach to improving your travel experience and making a positive impact on the places you visit is to support local communities. In Slovakia, aiding local communities takes on even greater significance since visitors are enthralled with the allure of regional customs and the friendliness of locals. The following are a few methods that you can:

1. Choose Locally-Owned Accommodations:
Choose locally owned boutique hotels, bed and breakfasts, or guesthouses. This guarantees that a large percentage of your lodging costs go directly toward supporting the neighborhood.

2. Visit local Markets to Shop:
Visit neighborhood markets to buy locally manufactured things, handcrafted items, and traditional items. This helps small companies and local craftspeople.

3. Eat at Nearby Eateries:
Select eateries that are owned and operated locally if you want to taste real Slovak food.

This promotes regional farmers, chefs, and the food scene as a whole.

4. Attend Festivals and Local Events: Take part in celebrations and events held locally. In addition to enhancing your experience, your presence supports the local economy in the area holding the event.

5. Employ Regional Guides: Take into account hiring local guides when visiting attractions or going on tours. They boost the local economy and offer insider information.

6. Invest in souvenirs and handicrafts: Spend money on trinkets and handicrafts created locally. This preserves original and genuine mementos while also promoting regional craftspeople and their customary methods of creation.

7. Engage in Activities Related to Responsible Tourism: Take part in eco-friendly tourist endeavors that put the health of nearby communities and ecosystems first. This could be community-led projects, eco-friendly excursions, or cultural events.

8. Encourage Social Entrepreneurs: Look for projects and social enterprises that support community development. This can entail lending a hand to companies that positively address environmental or social challenges.

9. Observe Regional Traditions and Customs:

Honor and value regional traditions and customs. Positive relationships are fostered when you recognize and respect the cultural quirks of the community you are visiting.

10. Stay in Rural Homestays:

Take into account booking an agritourism or rural guesthouse. Families in rural areas directly benefit from this and get an intimate view of local life.

11. Contribute Responsibly:

If you're interested in volunteering, look for positions with respectable groups that emphasize ethical and sustainable operations.

12. Reduce the Impact on the Environment:

Consider how your actions affect the environment. Reduce the amount of water you use, dispose of garbage properly, and support green projects that help protect the environment and the environment.

13. Partake in Intercultural Dialogue:

Be willing to share cultures. Engage in conversation with locals to exchange personal stories and learn about their everyday lives.

Mutual understanding is promoted and meaningful connections are made as a result.

14. Make Use of Local Transit:

Use public transportation, such as buses or trains, to get between locations. This lessens your environmental impact and supports the regional transportation system.

15. Post a Satisfied Review:

Write favorable feedback for the establishments, lodgings, and services you experienced after your visit. This draws additional customers to nearby companies.

You may actively contribute to the sustainability of tourist attractions, the empowerment of local economies, and the preservation of cultural treasures by deciding to support your community. You have the power to significantly impact the lives of those you come into contact with while visiting Slovakia.

10. Your Slovakian Itinerary

One Week in Slovakia: A Balanced Journey

A weeklong trip in Slovakia provides the ideal amount of immersive activities, natural beauty, and cultural exploration. This is a possible schedule for a week spent in Slovakia:

Days 1-2: The Charm of the Capital, Bratislava

Explore Old Town in the Morning

- Begin your adventure in the Old Town of Bratislava. Explore the cobblestone roads, stop at St. Michael's Gate, and be in awe of the unusual Cumil statue.

Riverfront and Bratislava Castle in the afternoon

- Visit Bratislava Castle for sweeping views of the Danube River and the city. Take a stroll around the riverfront and consider going on a boat excursion.

Evening: Old Town Dinner

- Savor a classic Slovak meal at one of Old Town's neighborhood eateries. Take in the vibrant ambiance and taste regional cuisine.

Day 3: The Little Rome, Trnava
Morning: Trnava's Historic Center
Trnava's Historic Center in the morning
See St. John the Baptist Cathedral, stroll around the historic center, and take in the stunning Renaissance architecture of Trnava, also called "The Little Rome."
Lunch and relaxation in the afternoon
- Enjoy lunch at a neighborhood cafe and spend some time unwinding in Trnava's serene atmosphere.
Evening: Local Flavors and Dinner
Savor dinner in a classic Slovak restaurant while discovering the distinctive local flavors of Trnava.
Day 4: Peaks and Trails in the High Tatras
Tours Poprad in the Morning
- Travel to Poprad, which is the High Tatras' entry point. Travel to the High Tatras by cable car or cogwheel train.
Afternoon: Adventure on the Cable Car or Hike
- To see stunning vistas of the mountains, select a hike that is appropriate for your level of fitness or ride the cable car.
Evening: Unwinding and Regional Food

In one of the mountain lodges, unwind amid the alpine ambiance while enjoying regional food.

Day 5: National Park of Slovak Paradise

Full Day: Adventure in Slovak Paradise

- Take a hike through the breathtaking gorges, waterfalls, and hiking paths of Slovak Paradise National Park. Take a climb on the renowned "Prielom Hornádu".

Afternoon: Head back to Poprad

Make your way back to Poprad for the night. Relax and think back on your travels during the day.

Day 6: Eastern Elegance in Košice

Discover Košice's Historic Center in the Morning

- Visit Slovakia's second-largest city, Košice. Discover the State Theatre and St. Elisabeth Cathedral in the quaint old center.

Lunch and Cultural Sites in the Afternoon

- Savor a midday meal at a neighborhood restaurant in Košice. See the famous singing fountain and the East Slovak Museum.

Košice by Night: Evening

- Take in Košice's colorful atmosphere throughout the night by taking a stroll down Hlavná Street.

Day 7: Mining Heritage in Banská Bystrica

Discover the City Center in the Morning

- Visit Banská Bystrica, a city renowned for its mining history. Take a tour of the city's core, which includes SNP Square.

Afternoon: Castle and Museum

- To gain an understanding of the history of the area, see Banská Bystrica Castle and the Slovak National Uprising Museum.

Farewell Dinner: Evening

- Enjoy a final meal at a neighborhood eatery while thinking back on your week-long exploration of Slovakia.

This program provides a well-rounded and unforgettable week in Slovakia by combining historical exploration, natural beauties, and local experiences. Adaptations might be made according to your individual preferences and the season you visit.

Extended Exploration: A Two-Week Adventure

You can get a deeper understanding of Slovakia's varied landscapes, rich cultural heritage, and hidden gems by extending your trip to two weeks. An itinerary for a longer trip is shown below:

Cultural Discovery in Week One

Days 1-4: Western Slovakia and Bratislava**

- Explore Bratislava and the surrounding areas during the first four days of the one-week excursion by following the plan.

Days 5-7: Čachtice Castle, Nitra, and Trenčín

- Travel to Nitra and see its historical landmarks. Travel to Trenčín and see the magnificent Trenčín Castle. Visit Čachtice Castle, a place with a fascinating past and a connection to the "Bloody Countess."

Days 8–10: Mining Towns, Donovaly, and Banska Bystrica

- Visit the historical hub of Banska Bystrica and the neighboring mining towns. For outdoor recreation and the allure of a mountain resort, travel to Donovaly.

Days 11–14: Eastern Slovakia and Košice

Travel to Košice and spend some time discovering the cultural attractions of the city, such as the distinctive Steel Arena, cathedrals, and museums. Explore the Tokaj wine area, which is close by and is renowned for its scenic wine cellars and vineyards.

Second Week: Adventure and Nature

High Tatras and Poprad: Day 15–17

- Head back to the High Tatras, paying particular attention to the area surrounding Poprad. Discover more hiking routes, pay a visit to Tatra National Park, and unwind in Aquacity Poprad's warm springs.

Days 18–20: Spiš Castle and Slovak Paradise National Park

- Take in the splendor of Slovak Paradise National Park by discovering new paths and scenic spots. Take a tour of Spiš Castle, one of Europe's biggest castle complexes.

Days 21–14: Orava Castle and Pieniny National Park

- Explore Pieniny National Park, which is well-known for the Gorge of the Dunajec River. Take a trip on a traditional raft. Take a look at Orava Castle, which is situated against Orava Lake.

More Advice:

- **Local Festivals & activities:** See what local celebrations and activities are scheduled for the time you will be there. Taking part in these cultural events will enrich your travels with unforgettable experiences.

Village Stays: Take into consideration spending a night or two in a traditional village, which provides an opportunity to help out local people and get a peek into rural Slovak life.

Local Markets: Visit local markets in different places to learn about handcrafted items, and local specialties, and to engage with merchants.

Hiking and Adventure Activities: Enjoy hiking, biking, and other adventure sports amidst Slovakia's varied landscapes. There are lots of possibilities for outdoor enthusiasts, from national parks to the Tatras.

Wine Tasting: If you're a wine enthusiast, visit Slovakia's wine areas, including the Small Carpathians and Tokaj, and partake in wine tastings.

Culinary Adventures: Sample local specialties and, if offered, enroll in cooking workshops to delve deeper into Slovak cuisine.

Always be adaptable with your ideas and welcome impromptu discoveries as you go. Slovakia's breathtaking scenery, kind people, and rich historical legacy make it the ideal location for a lengthy journey.

Customizing Your Experience

You can adjust your trip to Slovakia to fit your interests and preferences by personalizing your experience there. Here are some ideas for personalizing your Slovakian journey, regardless of your interests in history, the outdoors, adventure, or delicious food:

1. Culturally Inspired:

- **Longer City Touring:** Take extra time to visit Košice, Bratislava, and other historic cities. Explore museums, art galleries, and cultural events in depth.

- **Local Experiences:** To fully immerse oneself in Slovak culture, take part in local workshops, folk music concerts, or folk festivals.

- **Historical Villages:** Discover lesser-known historical villages with classic Slovak architecture, such as Špania Dolina or Vlkolínec.

2. A lover of nature:

Longer Stays in National Parks: Spend more time hiking, observing wildlife, and taking pictures of the natural world in the High Tatras, Slovak Paradise National Park, and Pieniny National Park.

- **Thermal Spas:** Unwind in the scenically surrounded thermal spas in Poprad, AquaCity, or other locations.

- **Amazing Views:** Don't miss excursions to viewpoints atop mountains, such as Lomnický štít or Chopok, for breathtaking sweeping vistas.

3. Seeker of Adventure:

Adventurous Activities: In the High Tatras or Slovak Paradise, partake in heart-pounding sports like zip-lining, rock climbing, and paragliding.

- **Caving Exploration:** Discover Slovakia's many caves, including the Domica Cave and the Demänovská Ice Cave.
- **Rafting and Kayaking:** Take advantage of river rafting or kayaking in places like Pieniny National Park's Dunajec River.

4. Explorer of Cooking:
- **Local cuisine excursions:** Sample street cuisine and regional specialties in towns like Bratislava and Košice by going on guided food excursions.
- **Wine Tasting:** Visit wine regions to sample wines in nearby vineyards, like Tokaj or the Small Carpathians.
- **Cooking Classes:** Take advantage of this opportunity to learn how to make authentic Slovak cuisine.

5. Inland Retreat:
- **Village Stays:** For a genuine rural experience, choose homestays or cozy guesthouses in charming villages like Čičmany or Zuberec.
- **Countryside Cycling:** Rent a bike and ride through picturesque towns and landscapes to get a taste of the Slovak countryside.
- **Agritourism Experiences:** Take part in agritourism pursuits like traditional crafts or farm work assistance.

6. Relaxation and well-being:

- Spa Retreat: Take some time to indulge in spa treatments and wellness getaways at places like Piestany or Bardejov.

- Yoga and Meditation: Look for retreats offering yoga and meditation in peaceful outdoor environments.

- Forest Bathing: Take advantage of Slovakia's verdant woodlands to indulge in the Japanese practice of "shinrin-yoku"

7. Photography Aficionado:

- Scenic Landscapes: Pay close attention to capturing the splendor of Slovakia's terrain, including the tranquil lakes and valleys and the rugged Tatra Mountains.

- Historic Architecture: Take pictures of old buildings in towns like Spišská Kapitula, Levoča, and Bardejov.

- Golden Hour Shots: For the best lighting, schedule your activities for just before or after dawn or sunset.

8. Winter Wonderland:

- Winter Sports: Go skiing, snowboarding, and winter trekking in the High Tatras or at ski areas like Jasná during the winter.

- Christmas Markets: Travel to cities like Bratislava and Košice to witness the enchantment of Slovak Christmas markets.

- Cozy Mountain Lodges: Surrounded by scenes blanketed in snow, stay in cozy mountain lodges.

9. Romantic Vacation:

Castle Stays: For a magical experience, the reserve stays in quaint castles like Bojnice Castle.

- Wine and Candlelight meals: Savor intimate candlelit meals and wine tastings on romantic evenings.

Experience the romantic Danube boat ride or one of the other beautiful rivers.

By tailoring your experience to your interests and passions, you may design a unique itinerary that will make your trip to Slovakia unforgettable.

11. Beyond Slovakia

Nearby Attractions

Slovakia is a country in Central Europe that borders numerous other nations, making it an ideal location for exploring neighboring sites. Here are some local locations you might think about including in your trip, depending on your interests:

1. Austria's Vienna:

Area of separation from Bratislava: Roughly 65 kilometers.

Travel time by train or automobile is approximately one hour.

- Highlights: Take in the lively cultural scene in Austria's capital while touring the imperial palaces and museums.

2. Hungary's Budapest:

The distance is roughly 200 kilometers from Bratislava.

- Destination Time: About 2.5 hours via automobile or rail.

- Highlights: Take a stroll along the Danube River, explore the old Buda Castle, and unwind in thermal springs.

3. Czech Republic, Prague:

Distance from Bratislava: About 330 kilometers

Travel Time: by train or automobile is approximately 3.5 hours.

- **Highlights:** Take in Prague's Old Town Square, Prague Castle, and the famous Charles Bridge to fully experience its medieval beauty.

4. Poland's Kraków:

Area of departure from Bratislava: Roughly 340 km.

Total Travel Time: Approximately 4 hours by automobile or rail.

- **Highlights:** Take a tour of the UNESCO-listed Wawel Castle, stroll around the ancient Old Town and stop by the nearby Auschwitz-Birkenau for some reflection.

5. Poland's Zakopane:

About 150 kilometers separate Poprad (High Tatras) from this location.

Travel time by car: around two hours.

- **Highlights:** Discover the quaint mountain village of Zakopane, which is well-known for its wood-framed buildings and proximity to the Tatra Mountains.

6. Poland's Wieliczka Salt Mine and Krakow:

- The distance is roughly 190 kilometers from Poprad (High Tatras).

Total Time: About two and a half hours by automobile.

- **Highlights:** Combine a trip to the UNESCO-designated Wieliczka Salt Mine with a visit to Kraków.

7. Poland's Wrocław:

- The distance is roughly 250 kilometers from Košice.

Travel time by car: around three hours.

- **Highlights:** Take in the city's architectural treasures, explore the lovely Old Town and pay a visit to the Wrocław Cathedral.

8. Lviv, Ukraine

- The distance is roughly 350 kilometers from Košice.

Travel time by car: around four hours.

- **Highlights:** Take in the distinctive cultural ambiance of Lviv, explore the UNESCO-listed Old Town, and tour historic cathedrals.

9. Germany's Dresden:

About 450 kilometers separate you from Bratislava.

Travel time by train or automobile is approximately 4.5 hours.

- **Highlights:** Take in the stunning old buildings in this Elbe River cultural center, including the Frauenkirche and Zwinger Palace.

10. From Poland's High Tatras to Zakopane:

- About 80 kilometers separate Poprad (High Tatras) from this location.
Travel time by car: around 1.5 hours.
- **Highlights:** Take in a breathtaking drive across the High Tatras to arrive at the quaint Polish mountain village of Zakopane.
Think about the duration of the trip, the need for a visa, and any other practicalities while organizing a visit to neighboring attractions. These adjacent locations provide a variety of activities, from natural beauty to historical exploration, enriching your trip across Central Europe.

Connecting Countries

You can explore other cultures, landscapes, and histories by connecting nations on your trip schedule, which offers a rich and varied experience. Here are some ideas for making connections between nations using Slovakia as a hub:
1. **Central European Exploration: Hungary, Austria, Slovakia, and the Czech Republic: ****
**Slovakia's Bratislava:
- Take a tour of Bratislava Castle and Old Town.
- Spend the day at Devin Castle.
- **Hungary, Budapest:**

- Visit Fisherman's Bastion, Buda Castle, and the hot springs.
- Take pleasure in a Danube River cruise.

- Austria, Vienna:
- See the Belvedere Palace and Schönbrunn Palace.
- Visit the many museums and the thriving cultural scene.

Czech Republic, Prague:
- Stroll around Prague's Old Town's quaint streets.
- See Charles Bridge and Prague Castle.

2. Travel Through Eastern Europe: Slovakia, Poland, and Ukraine:

Slovakia's Bratislava:
- Visit the museums and landmarks in the nation's capital.

Poland: Kraków:
- Take a tour of the ancient Old Town and Wawel Castle.
- Visit the Wieliczka Salt Mine for the day.

Poland's Zakopane:
- Take in Zakopane's mountain charm in the Tatra Mountains.

Ukraine, Lviv:
- Explore the historic cathedrals and Old Town, which is listed by UNESCO.

3. Alpine Travel: Austria - Germany - Slovakia:

Slovakia's Bratislava:
Start your trip in Bratislava.
- Austria, Vienna:
- Visit cultural landmarks and imperial palaces.
- Austria, Salzburg:
- See the Hohensalzburg Fortress and the birthplace of Mozart.
- Germany, Munich:
- Visit the Marienplatz, take in the architecture, and learn about Bavarian culture.
4. Exploration of the Transcarpathian Region: Slovakia, Hungary, Romania:
Slovakia's Bratislava:
Commence at the nation's capital.
- Hungary, Budapest:
- Visit Buda Castle and historical sites.
Bucharest, Romania:
Explore the thriving cultural landscape and pay a visit to St. Michael's Church.
- Republic of Sibu:
- See the Transylvanian heartland's medieval architecture.
5. Danube Delta Journey: Hungary, Serbia, Romania, Slovakia:
**Slovakia's Bratislava:
Start your trip in Bratislava.
- Hungary, Budapest:
- Take a Danube cruise or visit the city's attractions.

- Serbia, Belgrade:
- Take in the historical sites and thriving nightlife.

Moldova, Romania:
- Take a tour of the city's museums and the Palace of the Parliament.

6. Circuit of the Carpathian Mountains:

Slovakia, Poland, Romania:

Slovakia's Bratislava:
- Set out from the capital on your journey.

Poland's Zakopane:
- Take in the local way of life by exploring the Tatra Mountains.

Bucharest, Romania:
- Explore the center of Transylvania.

Romanian Braşov:
- See the Black Church and stroll through the old, medieval town.

With the variety of historic cities, picturesque scenery, and multicultural experiences these itineraries provide, you can design an unforgettable trip across Central and Eastern Europe. You can modify the length of time you spend at each location according to your tastes and interests.

Exploring the Heart of Europe

Traveling through nations like Slovakia which are located in central Europe provides an enthralling adventure through a wealth of cultural diversity, fascinating history, and stunning scenery. Here's a well-planned schedule to let you experience the spirit of Central Europe:

Days 1-3: Start in Slovakia's Bratislava**

- **Discover Old Town:** Stroll around the quaint alleyways, stop by St. Michael's Gate, and find the distinctive Cumil monument.

- **Bratislava Castle:** Take in expansive vistas of the Danube River and the city.

- **Danube Riverboat:** For an alternative viewpoint of the city, take a picturesque boat down the Danube River.

Budapest, Hungary (Days 4-6)

- **Buda Castle:** Take a tour of the ancient Buda Castle grounds.

- **Fisherman's Bastion:** From this famous terrace, take in expansive views of Budapest.

- **Thermal Baths:** Unwind in the well-known Széchenyi or Gellért Baths.

- **Danube Promenade:** Cross the Chain Bridge and stroll along the Danube Promenade.

Days 7-9: Austria's Vienna

- **Schönbrunn residence:** Explore the magnificent gardens and residence of the imperial family.

Explore the famous art museum housed in a stunning royal complex at Belvedere Royal.

The St. Stephen's Cathedral: Take in the views from the tower and the building's architecture.

- **Vienna Woods:** Spend a day exploring the natural and cultural treasures of Vienna Woods.

Prague, Czech Republic, Days 10–12

- **Prague Castle:** Explore the world's largest ancient castle.

- **Charles Bridge:** Cross this famous bridge that links Prague Castle with Old Town.

- **Old Town Square:** Take in the vibrant environment, stop by the Astronomical Clock, and browse the neighborhood shops.

- **Vltava River Cruise:** Sail down the Vltava River in comfort.

Days 13–15: Poland's Kraków

- **Wawel Castle:** Take a tour of the ancient fortress situated beside the Vistula River.

- **Old Town:** Take a stroll through Kraków's Old Town's quaint streets.

- **Auschwitz-Birkenau:** Visit the concentration camp for a sobering yet crucial day trip.

- **Wieliczka Salt Mine:** Explore this UNESCO-listed salt mine that has sculptures and underground chambers.

Days 16–18: Poland's Tatra Mountains and Zakopane**

- **Discover Zakopane:** Take in Zakopane's mountain charm in the Tatra Mountains.
- **Tatra National Park:** Enjoy the breathtaking alpine scenery by hiking or riding the cable car.
- **Chocholowska Valley:** Take a stroll through this charming valley home to wooden cottages.

Days 19–21: Go back to Slovakia's Bratislava

- **Final Hours in Bratislava:**Go back to your favorite locations or check out any sights you may have missed.

Woodland Park of Bratislava: Enjoy a stroll through this vast woodland park.

- **Goodbye Dinner:** Savor a goodbye meal at one of the quaint eateries in Bratislava.

More Advice:

- **Local Experiences:** Take advantage of local experiences on your travels, such as sampling regional cuisine, going to cultural events, or taking part in seminars.
- **Transportation:** Trains and buses provide handy connections as well as beautiful itineraries when traveling between cities.
- **Cultural Events:** To add a cultural component to your trip, look for festivals or events taking place in the cities you intend to visit.

This itinerary offers a thorough overview of the core of Europe by fusing the attraction of historic cities, cultural diversity, and breathtaking scenery. Adapt the length of your stay at each location to your interests and speed of travel.

12. Conclusion

Reflecting on Your Journey

As your tour to Slovakia, Austria, Hungary, the Czech Republic, and Poland draws to a finish, pause to consider the memories, learning opportunities, and personal development you've had. The following can help you think back on your 21-day journey:

1. Treasured Times:

- **Highlight Reel:** Think back on the highlights of your trip that left a lasting impression. It might be an amazing vista, a cross-cultural interaction, or an unanticipated finding.

2. Cultural Perspectives:

- **Cultural Learnings:** Consider the various civilizations you have come across. Which novel habits, traditions, or regional behaviors piqued your interest the most?

3. Personal Development:

- **Difficulties Overcome:** Reflect on any difficulties you encountered traveling. What did you discover about yourself while navigating them, and how did you do it?

4. Links Established:

- **Persons Met:** Consider the persons you came into contact with during your journey.

Was there a specific interaction that made a lasting impression? In what ways did these connections improve your trip?

5. Beauty of Nature:

- **Scenic Wonders:** Reflect on the wild settings you experienced. What effects did these settings have on your general well-being and mental state?

6. Gourmet Highlights:

- **Tastes and Flavors:** Remember the gastronomic adventures. Which foods were your favorites, and did you taste any unexpected local specialties?

7. Immersion in History:

- **Historical Marvels:** Reflect on the historical locations you have visited. Did any particular historical setting or narrative strike a chord with you?

8. Nature's Insight:

- **Silent Times:** Ponder the times when you were alone, whether it was a serene lake, a peaceful mountain top, or a peaceful forest. In what way did these moments help you reflect?

9. Cultural Different

- **Differences Between Cities:** Examine the ambiances and feelings of the different places you went. What aspects of the ambiance, architecture, and culture were unique to each location?

10. Acquired Knowledge:

- **Travel Insights:** Consider the knowledge you have acquired from your experience. Which lessons are you going to apply to your day-to-day activities?

11. upcoming investigations:

- **Next Adventure:** Ponder the next destination your wanderlust may take you. Based on this voyage, are there any additional areas or nations that you would like to explore?

12. Thank You:

- **Grateful Moments:** Give thanks for the encounters, the individuals you got to know, and the chances that presented themselves. What has brought you the most gratitude on this journey?

13. Storing Recollections:

- **Recording Your Travels:** Examine any diaries, pictures, or mementos you have accumulated so far. How are you going to share and preserve these memories?

14. Getting Ready for the Future:

Travel Aspirations: In light of your reflections, are there any particular facets you'd like to delve deeper into or include in your upcoming travels?

15. Closing Chapter:

- **Concluding Remarks:** As you say goodbye to this leg of your journey, what feelings and ideas are still present? For you, what signifies the conclusion of this journey?

Reflecting on your trips helps you to better understand yourself and the world around you, as well as to plan for future adventures and experiences. It also solidified the influence of your travels.

Your Next Adventure Awaits!

Remember that your next adventure awaits as you wrap up your incredible tour across the heart of Europe, full of natural beauty, cultural treasures, and life-changing experiences! The world is full of opportunities, regardless of your ambition to go to new places, learn about other cultures, or have exciting adventures. This manual will help you plan your next adventure:

1. Explore Unspoiled Terrains:

- Recommended Locations:

- Patagonia, Argentina, and Chile: Discover breathtaking glaciers, highlands, and secluded settings.

- Canada's Banff National Park: Take in the unspoiled splendor of the Canadian Rockies.

- Iceland: Take in the surreal scenery of waterfalls, volcanoes, and glaciers.

2. Cultural Encounter:

- Recommended Locations:

Visit historic temples and tea ceremonies to fully immerse yourself in traditional Japanese culture in Kyoto, Japan.

- Marrakech, Morocco: Immerse yourself in the country's colorful marketplaces, storied palaces, and rich customs.
- Jaipur, India: Discover the Pink City's palaces, forts, and cultural legacy.

3. Experimentation and Excitation:
- Recommended Locations:

- Queenstown, New Zealand: Take part in adventure sports in breathtaking scenery.
- Interlaken, Switzerland: Immerse yourself in outdoor pursuits amid the breathtaking Swiss Alps.

Costa Rica: Take pleasure in surfing, zip-lining, and exploring verdant rainforests.

4. Historical Expeditions:
- Recommended Locations:

- Rome, Italy: Discover the past of the Vatican City and the Roman Empire.
- Athens, Greece: Discover the ancient ruins of the birthplace of Western civilization.
- Cairo, Egypt: Explore the wonders of the Sphinx and pyramids, as well as the history of ancient Egyptian culture.

5. Island Getaways:
- Recommended Locations:

- Santorini, Greece: Unwind on gorgeous beaches, see quaint towns, and take in breathtaking sunsets.
- Bora Bora, French Polynesia: Stay in overwater bungalows for luxury and peace.
- Maldives: Take a plunge into pristine seas and savor the peace of remote islands.

6. Urban Investigation:
- Recommended Locations:
Tokyo, Japan: Immerse yourself in the cutting-edge street life, technology, and futuristic cityscape.
- New York City, USA: Discover the city's recognizable sites, varied neighborhoods, and cultural establishments.
- Barcelona, Spain: Take in the colorful street markets, Antoni Gaudí architecture, and the Mediterranean ambiance.

7. Wildlife Meetings:
- Recommended Locations:
- Galápagos Islands, Ecuador: Take in the distinctive fauna in its native environment.
- Tanzania's Serengeti National Park: Witness the Great Migration and a variety of African fauna.
- Amazon Rainforest, Brazil: Discover the world's largest rainforest's abundant biodiversity.

8. Relaxation Getaways:

- Recommended Locations:

- Bali, Indonesia: In a tropical paradise, embrace holistic wellness techniques.
- Tuscany, Italy: Incorporate delicious food, beautiful scenery, and wellbeing.

Costa Rica: Rejuvenate yourself in natural, eco-friendly getaways.

9. Road Trip Experiences:
- Recommended Locations:

- Pacific Coast Highway, United States: Travel the breathtaking California coast.
- Iceland's Ring Road: Discover the whole island, from glaciers to waterfalls.
- Australia's Great Ocean Road offers breathtaking coastline views, abundant animals, and well-known landmarks.

10. Festivals of Culture:
- Recommended Locations:

- Rio de Janeiro, Brazil: Take part in the colorful Carnival festivities.

Kyoto, Japan: During Hanami season, take in the splendor of the cherry blossoms.

- Edinburgh, Scotland: Take in the famous Fringe of the Edinburgh Festival.

Your next journey is a blank canvas just waiting for you to fill it with new encounters, relationships, and learnings. I hope your journey through wanderlust is full of adventure, personal development, and the delight of discovery. I hope your next great adventure takes you safely.

Made in United States
Troutdale, OR
07/12/2024

21190091R10096